The Essence

FLY FISHING

Donald Downs, Taff Price,
Dr R. J. Roberts, Wilson Stephens,
Philip Tallents, John Veniard,
Conrad Voss Bark, Dermot Wilson

BARRY SHURLOCK

BARRY SHURLOCK
& Co. (Publishers) Ltd
174 Stockbridge Road,
WINCHESTER
Hants, SO22 6RW

First published 1976

ISBN 0 903330 25 3

Reproduced and printed by photolithography
and bound in Great Britain at The Pitman
Press, Bath

Contents

R. J. Roberts

The Fish: Natural History of the Salmonids

Trout and salmon belong to the salmonid family of fishes. Although considered by many fishermen to be superior to the so-called coarse fish, in evolutionary terms they are in fact more primitive. As the name implies they are the fish of the salmon family which of course includes the Atlantic salmon and the Pacific salmon and also the brown trout and rainbow trout, so keenly sought after by the fly fisherman. It also includes some species of white fish — the powan of Loch Lomond, pollan of Loch Neagh, vendance of Loch Maben and gwyniad of Llyn Tegid — which are closely related to the game fish familiar to the fly fisherman, and to prove it carry the mark of the salmonid, a little adipose fin immediately in front of the tail. The fly angler is, however, most unlikely to capture them, or even to notice their existence, despite their presence in vast shoals, as they feed on minute planktonic animals. The coregonids, as these white fish are called, are themselves closely related to the grayling, a species midway between them and the salmon. The grayling is called *Thymallus thymallus* by the zoologists and this is a very appropriate name, since when it is first captured it has a distinct fragrance of thyme. The grayling is also capable of providing superb sport for the fly angler in winter, when fishing for other game fish is restricted by the close season.

The names salmon and trout are not really reliable as indicators of the relationships within the genus since many of the species called trout by the American fishermen are in fact char, so the brook trout, Dolly Varden trout, and cut-throat trout are not really trout at all. Similarly, the giant *Hucho hucho* trout of the Danube is also a char. Even more confusing, the so-called rock-salmon is not a salmon, or even a true fish — it is the fishmonger's disguise for dogfish, a shark.

Which species, then, fall properly into this group of genuine trout and salmon, the fly-angler's master race? In fact there are relatively few true species although variants associated with geographical isolation are sometimes graced with invalid titles such as Loch Leven trout or fario trout.

THE SALMONIDS

The Atlantic salmon, so aptly called the leaping salmon, *Salmo salar*, is the best known and most prized species and is found in rivers running into the Atlantic Ocean on both the European and American continents. In Europe its range extends as far south as Portugal and as far north as the Arctic Coast of Russia, but in America the southern limits of that range are somewhat more restricted, comprising from Ungava in Northern Canada to the Connecticut river.

In the Pacific, instead of one species of salmon, there are at least six species, all closely related but with different life cycles and often very different in shape and colour. These species are called *Oncorhynchus* — 'the one with the hooked nose' — and comprise *O. masou* which is a Japanese species, *O. kisutch*, the coho salmon, which is prized by sea anglers and is found in Japan and, like most of the other species, all down the Western seaboard of America from Alaska to California. *O. keta*, the dog or chum salmon, is a small species which, at spawning, has a fearsome array of canine teeth and has a range similar to that of the coho. *Oncorhynchus tshawytscha* is the biggest of all the salmonids. It is known as the chinook or king salmon, and may weigh almost 50 kg (over 100 lbs). *Oncorhynchus nerka* is very familiar to all British anglers as it is the fish which fills the tins of 'Red-Alaska sockeye salmon' which is so common in grocers' shops.

Oncorhynchus gorbuscha the hump back, or pink salmon was originally confined to the same Pacific range as the others but recently individual fish of this species have been turning up in nets off the Scottish Coast and in a number of salmon rivers. As usual the explanation for this mystery revolves around man's proclivity for transferring fish from one river to another. In this case Russian scientists had transferred large numbers of eggs of this and of other Pacific salmon species from rivers in Soviet Asia to rivers of the White Sea and there is now an established stock of these rather ugly, very hump-backed salmon in the Atlantic. It is not yet known whether the other Pacific salmon species transferred have successfully established themselves.

It is not usually difficult to distinguish Atlantic salmon from

Pacific salmon when they are in their spawning livery, since the latter are very brightly coloured on the spawning gravel. However, at younger stages, or in the sea, they may look more alike and may be confused now that Pacific salmon also occur in Atlantic waters. Generally speaking, the way that zoologists distinguish between the two is by counting the number of rays, or supports, in the anal fin and by counting the number of gill-rakers on the outer gill arch. Gill-rakers are the small white tooth-like processes arrayed along the free edge of the supporting arch of the gill. Atlantic salmon have 12 or less anal fin rays, and 20 or less gill-rakers whereas Pacific salmon have 13 or more anal fin rays and up to 40 gill-rakers.

The Life Cycle of the Salmon

The major mysteries of the life cycle of the Atlantic salmon have only recently been completely unravelled and there are still many gaps in our knowledge. Although the stages when the fish lives in fresh water have been relatively accessible to investigation it is only by extensive marking and recapture of marked fish that their migration routes and feeding zones in the Atlantic Ocean and, in the case of Baltic fish, in the Gulfs of Bothnia and Finland, have been discovered. The method of marking used is called tagging and involves the attachment of a small plastic label to the fish by means of a surgical stitch inserted through the back muscle. Usually instructions as to where to send any recaptured fish are printed on the tag and anglers catching such fish are performing a real service to biological science if they submit them to the laboratory as requested.

The Atlantic salmon spends the first part of its life in the river in which it is born. The female lays her ova, large orange pearl-like eggs, in a hollow in the stream bed known as a redd. The male squeezes a cloud of milt over them, which rapidly fertilises them and then the female covers them with stones by flapping the redd with her tail. Occasionally a very small, precociously mature male parr may sneak in and join in the fertilisation ritual, so that if the adult male happens to be infertile, some of the eggs will still be successfully impregnated by this younger salmon.

The eggs are laid in groups of 2—300 in October—November, and usually hatch in Britain in March or April, although since the time of incubation is dependent on temperature, in colder countries such as Canada, Greenland or Sweden, the adult fish reach the spawning beds much earlier, before the ice freezes the rivers over, and do not hatch until the following June. The eggs are usually at

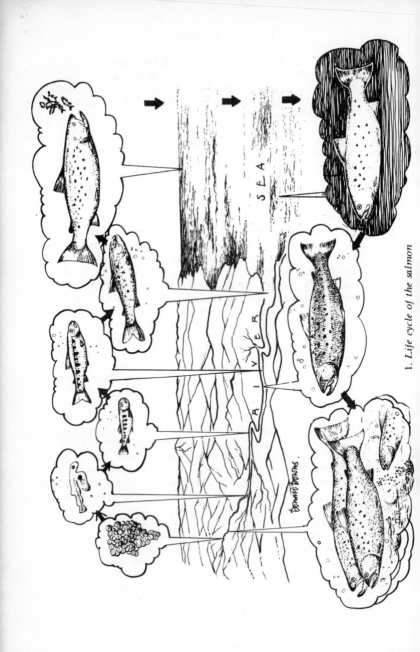

1. *Life cycle of the salmon*

least a foot down in the gravel, and immediately after laying is complete the number of redds in a river can be counted because the hummocks of clean gravel heaped over them by the female are obvious. Once the winter floods have passed, however, these hummocks are flattened and are no longer recognisable. By this time the eggs may only be 6—9 inches from the surface. The characteristics of the gravel, especially pebble size, are very important to allow free flow of oxygen-bearing water past the eggs, and anything which inhibits this, such as silt, can kill.

The young fish hatches into a bizarre, very vulnerable alevin, which is about 1″ long. It is hampered in its movements by a large orange balloon-like sac below its abdomen, known as the yolk sac. As the alevin, whose mouth and gills do not work at this stage, grows, it breathes through its skin and withdraws nutrients from the yolk sac which gradually shrinks until it merges with the abdominal wall. During this time, when it is defenceless and very vulnerable to predatory Caddis flies, Stoneflies or even its own older relations, the alevin stays down in the gravel of its redd, but once its yolk sac is resorbed, its mouth and gills functioning, and its shape more like that of a normal fish, it moves out of the gravel and starts to feed on any small moving prey on the gravel. Once its swim bladder has developed, the young fish, by this time known as a fry, can maintain its bouyancy at any level in the water and it moves off the gravel to feed to a large extent on insects drifting downstream in the water throughout the head waters of the river. Once the summer months arrive, they grow well and the largest could reach 3 or 4 inches by the onset of winter and are then called parr. They do not feed very much during the winter but the largest may move down river and feed avidly the following spring. A proportion of the parr, especially in the warmer parts of the salmon's range, are big enough by May of the year after their birth to go off to sea, but in Northern waters the majority have to spend two, three or even more years in fresh water to reach the necessary size. As already indicated quite a large proportion of the males become sexually mature even at this early stage.

When a parr decides to leave the river it migrates towards the sea and in the process it undergoes a profound physiological change. The skin becomes more delicate, and silvery pigments are deposited in it so that the colour of the fish changes from the brown, speckled pattern with its series of distinctive 'fingerprints' or 'parr-marks' to a typical sea type colour of blue—black above and white below, and the gills develop the capacity to breathe and excrete in salt water. The process is known as smoltification.

These young smolts congregate in the estuary of the river, and then set off for the major feeding grounds, feeding avidly and growing rapidly. Tagging experiments have shown that those fish which return after spending one winter at sea (grilse) feed off the Faroese coast but the big salmon, which spend two or more winters at sea and grow to a very large size — up to 60—70 lbs — travel to the waters off the West Coast of Greenland where vast shoals of them congregate from European and American stocks. Most of the Atlantic salmon from rivers entering the Baltic do not take part in these oceanic migrations, preferring instead to feed in the more productive areas of the Baltic itself, in the Gulfs of Bothnia and Finland. Consequently Atlantic and Baltic stocks virtually never mix.

At some stage, on the feeding ground, the salmon gets the urge to return home. We do not know what simulates this homing reaction, and we are unable to determine why some salmon return after one winter at sea and others may stay two or more. Certainly heredity plays a part, but environment must also be significant since a far higher proportion of salmon originating in long rivers return as salmon rather than grilse (one winter at sea) than is the case with fish originating from small spate streams.

The homing journey is very remarkable; we do not know how the fish finds its way from as far away as Greenland to the neighbourhood of its own river although presumably some method of navigation via the stars, similar to that of bird migration is used, but once the fish arrives off its home river its remarkably acute sense of smell seems to control its path. A salmon can recognise, by means of its nostrils, not only its own river, but even its own small tributary. Exactly what constitutes the stimulus which it recognises is not known for certain but current research suggests that pheromones — chemical signals produced by the young fish of its own spawning beds — passed down in the water of the river, are its underwater signposts. In Sweden and certain other areas where there are large hydro-electric dams blocking the upward migration of salmon, there are usually salmon rearing stations below the dams and salmon which emanate from these stations, not only return to the home river, but, so precise is their location ability, they actually attempt to jump up the effluent pipes from their farm of origin.

Salmon move into the rivers from the sea in any month of the year, but more especially when water flows are high and the temperature has risen above freezing. Spring salmon entering over the winter and early spring and having, in some instances, more than a year in which to reach the redds are usually rather reluctant to move upstream until water levels are high (usually associated with a rise in water temperature) — indeed some may well move downstream as often as they move upstream. On the other hand, fish entering fresh water during the summer and autumn have less time to spend on their journey, are nearer to sexual maturation, and consequently run upstream when water levels are lower. During the upstream migration the salmon lose their beautiful seagoing livery and revert to the brown colour of the parr. The sex hormones which are starting to circulate in greater levels as the ovary or testis develops, also affect other organs so that the secondary sexual characteristics of the spawning fish gradually develop. These include increased thickness of the skin, changes in the consistency of the external mucus and the development of the characteristic hooked jaw or 'kype' of the sexually mature male. The male also becomes red brown in colour, while the female remains a dull grey.

On the spawning bed the female commences redd digging, the male is attracted to the site and the cycle begins again. Once they have spawned the parents usually die, but some survive and as 'well-mended kelts' pass down the river again to the sea where they feed again and may return to spawn after a few months or a complete year. Fish which spawn more than once are not a very large proportion of a run of fish in the river, and three or more spawnings are very rare. The record, six spawnings, is held by a fish in the river Awe, Argyllshire, which was caught on the way to its seventh spawning. All Pacific salmon die after spawning.

Excluding the grilse, which are usually running at maximum levels in July, the runs of salmon in fresh water have three peaks coinciding with the spring, summer and autumn salmon. The spring salmon (remember salmon are those fish which have spent more than one winter at sea) may come into the river at any time from October to April and those coming into the river in November and December may be in the river for a full year without feeding before spawning.

THE TROUTS

The true species of trout are only two in number, the brown trout, *Salmo trutta*, and the rainbow trout, *Salmo gairdneri*.

The brown trout is very widely dispersed. Its natural range is Europe and the cooler areas around the Mediterranean, Black and Caspian seas. In addition, man's propensity for introducing fish to new waters, coupled with the extreme desirability of the species for sport and food, have resulted in its being naturalised in Australasia, higher areas of East, Central and Southern Africa, North and South America and the highlands of Kashmir, Assam, etc. in the Indian sub-continent.

The sea-trout is considered by many anglers to be a very different fish from the brown trout of lakes and rivers. Indeed, in law both in England and Scotland, it is classed with the salmon, rather than the trout, but biologically it is merely a brown trout which has chosen the sea as its feeding grounds and because of the richness of that feeding it is able to grow much faster than its entirely freshwater brothers. The seagoing trait is hereditary and even if prevented for a couple of generations from going to sea it appears to be retained.

Other varieties which have been claimed include Loch Leven trout, fario trout, ferox trout and lacustris trout but these again are all races of the same species and often the apparent differences are purely environmental. For instance the distinctive characteristics of Loch Leven trout, their red flesh and silvery colour with red spots, are completely lost when they are moved to another lake with a less suitable food supply.

The rainbow trout is sometimes called *Salmo irideus* which would be a good name because it emphasises one of the characteristic features of the species, the beautiful iridescent sheen along the flanks which is such a feature of the newly caught fish, but in biology the name which is first allotted to a species is sacrosanct, so *S. gairdneri* it must stay.

The rainbow is a relative newcomer to Europe. It was originally found in the rivers and streams of the Western American Coast flowing into the Pacific, especially the rivers of California, and there are two local varieties, the Shasta and Kamloops, named after two of the main rivers containing rainbows. Eggs from both of these varieties were introduced into Britain in the nineteenth century, notably by Sir James Maitland, who established the Howietoun fish hatchery and distributed eggs from these stocks, and from brook trout and other exotic species, all over the world. The Danish fish farming industry was also established around this time, and eggs from these Danish fish now provide most of our British rainbow trout for sport fisheries. So great has been the mixing of fish from the different rivers that it is now impossible to rationalise them into their original strains.

Although attempts have been made to naturalise stocks of rainbow trout in British waters, there is only one area, in Derbyshire, where incontrovertible evidence for a self-sustaining stock is available. Elsewhere stocks have to be maintained by restocking with farmed fish.

In its native waters the rainbow trout has, like the brown trout, a seagoing variant which spends a variable time in its river of birth before moving to the sea to feed. It is known as the steelhead trout, but it is otherwise indistinguishable from the freshwater rainbow trout and readily interbreeds with it.

Movements of Trout

The sea-trout and its American West coast cousin the steelhead have a very similar life cycle to that of the salmon but the journeys they undertake are less extensive, the majority preferring to feed in coastal waters much closer to their home river. Some sea-trout, known as finnock, return to fresh water in the same year as they migrate to the sea and these fish can also move in and out of other rivers (which is why they are often blamed for transmitting diseases like UDN between rivers). The finnock may start to enter fresh water from early autumn but the bigger, main run of spawning fish move into fresh water from May onwards. Sea-trout usually spawn more than once and there are records of sea-trout which have spawned 12 times.

During mid-summer, and later, both trout and salmon tend to run freely whenever there is a reasonable level of water. At earlier times of year they are less keen to run, and skulk in deep pools in the river, or at sea move up and down the coastline in shoals, waiting for spate conditions. Temperature is one of the most significant factors influencing movements of salmon and sea-trout. Low temperatures, especially near freezing, are especially important in inhibiting fish movements. Off-shore winds and cloud cover may also reduce the movements of fish although there will usually be some movements of rainbow trout in the first hours of darkness.

The movement of trout in rivers and lochs has been the subject of considerable investigation at the Freshwater Biological Association laboratories at Windermere and also in Scotland where scientists have tracked the movements of the fish by means of a small sonar tag inserted into the back of the fish. The tag is powered by a hearing aid battery and can be modified to indicate when the fish is feeding and how often it breathes. This work has shown that there are, every day, major periods of movement and feeding activity at sunrise and sunset, with small fish being less liable to confine themselves to these times. There is also a variable movement of feeding fish around noon, but these restricted times for movements are quite capable of being overridden by the eager feeding activities of the fish when there is a heavy hatch of large flies such as mayflies or Stoneflies.

The freshwater trouts, brown trout in Britain and rainbow in America, often use the lower reaches of the river, or a lake, as their growing grounds, to which they drop down after a year in the spawning tributaries, running up again to spawn when they are two or three years old. In lakes where there is no incoming stream suitable for spawning the adults may dig redds around the sides of the lake itself but because of the still water these are less well oxygenated than a stream redd and hence the success of such spawnings is limited.

SCALE READING

Much of the knowledge we have of the life cycle of salmonid fishes is based on the finding that all of this family carries its vital statistics on its back in the form of a detailed record of its age and growth rate inscribed on its scales. When a fish is fully scaled, it does not increase the number of scales as it grows. Instead the scales grow in size as the fish grows. The scales grow by addition of calcium matrix to its edge and this growth is usually directly proportional to the overall growth rate of the fish.

The surface of the scale is raised to form circuli and since circuli are laid down in a regular timescale, it follows that when growth of the fish is rapid then the distance between adjacent rings is greater than when growth is slow. Rapid growth takes place in the sea, and especially in summer, when food is more abundant. Consequently the scales of all salmonids show alternating bands of close and widely separated circuli. The close rings correspond to winter growth and the wide ones to summer growth. Fish which move to the sea grow very rapidly so that the period of their life spent in the sea in summer will be marked by especially distant rings, and even winter growth-rings in the sea may be as widely separated as the freshwater summer rings.

A year is represented on the scales by an area of closed and open bands. Thus the counting of these bands allows the biologist to estimate the age of the fish. Distinction between narrow summer and wide summer bands allows differentiation of life in the spawning stream and in the loch or low river, for trout or periods spent in freshwater and salt water for salmon and sea-trout. When a salmonid is maturing to spawn it stops feeding and especially in the male, material from the edge of the scale is resorbed to help nourish the gonad. This is never replaced exactly so that when regrowth commences there is a ragged edge or 'scar' on the scale which indicates a period spent in freshwater usually culminating in a spawning.

The combination of the results of scale reading and the various
national tagging and marking programmes has been instrumental
in allowing us to obtain virtually all of our present
knowledge of salmon biology. Much more information, especially
on migration patterns in the sea, is still required and this is
presently the subject of several research projects. Tagging projects
depend on an accurate return of captured tags by anglers and
commercial fishermen and as will be readily appreciated from the
above discussion of scale reading it is extremely useful for the
salmon or trout biologist to have a few scales from any recaptured
tagged fish. These can readily be removed by scraping the skin
(from tail to head), especially in the shoulder region, and placing
the mixture of skin and scales in an envelope to dry out. The sex,
length and weight of the fish, site of capture and lure should be
written on the envelope, and the scales and tag returned to the
laboratory named on the tag. Usually the sender will receive a small
monetary reward, together with details of the previous history of
his fish.

ANATOMY OF THE SALMONID

The successful trout or salmon angler usually has the job of
eviscerating his fish prior to cooking and this task can often be a
rewarding one in helping the understanding of the biology of his
quarry. When gutting a fish the angler should note any external
blemishes, any parasites on gills or body, and once the abdomen is
opened, recognise each organ as he removes it and make an
assessment of its health, nutritional status and presence of
parasites. The sex of the fish and state of maturity (size) of the
gonads should also be noted in the catch record as this helps
compare management techniques from one fishery to another and
from one year to another.

The general anatomy of a salmonid is shown in fig. 1. The
external features to note are the mouth, with its sharp backward
pointing teeth; the eye, which does not have eyelids; the nostrils
with their transverse flaps; the opercula covering the gill chambers,
and the lateral line. The simple arrangement of fins — paired
pectorals and pelvics, and dorsal and adipose (the small fatty 'fin' in
front of the tail) is characteristic of all salmonids. The fin rays, the
supporting ribs and the fins and tail, are soft and pliable. This is a
feature of the lower fishes and is very distinctive when compared
with the rigid and spiny fin rays of species like for instance the
perch.

The gills are the equivalent of the lungs and are very delicate indeed. Their red colour is due to blood which passes through them, picking up oxygen on its way and unloading carbon dioxide. The heart of the fish is enclosed in a rigid bony girdle below the gills and between the pectoral fins. It has a bright red contractile part and a white cone. In a newly killed fish, the heart will often continue to beat for many minutes.

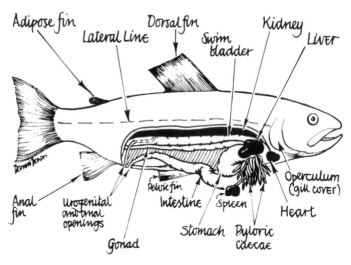

2. *Anatomy of a large male brown trout*

The digestive system of the salmonids, which are carnivores, is a relatively simple tube compared with that of an omnivorous species like the carp. From the mouth the oesophagus carries food to the stomach, which is where 'chewing' begins, since fish teeth are used purely for grasping. After digestion by the acids of the stomach and its strong muscles, food passes into the intestine, a long tube eventually ending in the anus. At the junction between the stomach and intestine there are a number of blind ending tubes, the pyloric caeca, which in a normal fish, are surrounded by white fat. In a very poor fish these can often be mistaken for parasitic worms sticking to the stomach wall. The liver is a soft flabby organ attached to the front of the stomach. In farmed fish freshly released into a fishery the liver may be a pasty yellow colour but once it gets wild food it soon regains its red brown colour. The gall bladder is a small balloon-like sac on the surface of the liver. It contains a greenish clear fluid, the bile.

The gonads — ovary and testis — are very insignificant structures unless the fish is developing to sexual maturity. The two ovaries of the female are fibrous sacs containing several thousand orange eggs. As they are ready to be laid the eggs break out of the sacs and lie free in the abdominal cavity. The testes of the male fish are two white sacs which extend the length of the cavity. At spawning they are very large and flabby.

Between the gonads and the backbone lie two structures which most anglers have seen but few know about. The first of these is the swim bladder. This is a buoyancy organ which is like a white sausage-shaped balloon. The fish can suck in air to the sac by means of the pneumatic duct — a small tube connecting the sac to the throat. The swim bladder allows the fish to maintain whatever level it requires, in the water, without wasting energy swimming. The other structure, hard up against the backbone, is often considered by the angler to be merely clotted blood, with a particularly black colour. It is in fact the kidney. Fish do not have hollow bones so that they cannot keep blood forming cells in their bone marrow and have to keep them in between the tubes of the long thin kidney, hence the dark colour. But fish kidneys do not function like those of mammals, which excrete the ammoniacal waste products of metabolism. Instead these are excreted via the gills, and in the sea, where the only water available for drinking is salt water, the salt taken into the body is also excreted through the gill tissues.

The muscle of fish is laid down in parallel wedge-shaped blocks, the myotomes, which all eventually pull on the tail, which is the main propulsive organ. These muscles are known as 'white' muscles and do not work by the normal method of oxygen metabolism as in higher animals. However along the line of the middle of the fish, on either side, is a strip of 'red' muscle which does function like our own muscles. When a game fish is merely swimming along he only uses his strips of red muscle but if severely frightened, as he is when being played by an angler, he uses all of the myotome muscles. Unfortunately for the fish, once these muscles have run out of energy they require hours to recharge and so the fish is 'played-out'. This is the stage when the angler reaches for the net or gaff. A fish which escapes at this late stage is liable to fall to the bottom and gasp for several hours before recovery.

The lateral line, which is the conspicuous demarcation of the upper and lower parts of the fish, and overlies the stripe of red muscle, is really a very complex sensory organ which senses vibrations in the water and warns of a boat or predator, or the nearby movement of a possible prey. The nostril is the other distinctive sensory organ on the outside of the fish. A paired organ, it is a blind sac with a bunch of finger-shaped sensory organelles with a direct nervous connection to the forebrain. There is a flap at the entrance to the nostril which directs water over the sensory tissue as the fish swims along. The dependence of the salmonids on their sense of smell to achieve their very exact homing runs means that the nostril has to be highly efficient and scientists have found that if they occlude the flow of water over the nostril by means of vaseline plugs then the fish does not manage to home, and merely swims about aimlessly until the spawning urge directs it to any spawning stream.

The brain of the salmon or trout is not as highly developed as the unsuccessful angler would suspect. In fact they are largely creatures of reflex and the largest areas of their brains are concerned with vision, smell and muscular co-ordination, with only a very minute amount of 'thinking' tissue.

VISION

The eye of the trout or salmon is very acute. They are fish that hunt by sight, but we should not assume that they see what we see in the same way. A fish below an object merely sees it as a dark shape against the sky unless it is silvery and therefore reflects light back to the fish, in which case the fish will not see it at all. This is why most fishes have white or silvery camouflaged undersides. But when looking directly at an object, the colour the fish sees will be largely dependent on the characteristics of the water. Usually in fresh water all colours become reddish-brown tinged and hence a salmon tag of a red colour will in theory be the least likely to attract fish. The red of the Bloody Butcher or Peter Ross fly will be seen as a dull orange, but since the red breast of a male stickleback also appears like this the trout will be attracted. In the sea all colours take on a blue-green tinge and blues are the least easily distinguished — which doesn't explain why the Blue Teal and Silver is such a successful fly for sea-trout in estuarine water!

The numerous occasions on which a fish rises short, or boils at a fly, i.e. touches or snaps at it and gets off, have encouraged anglers to recommend contact lenses for the fish! In fact the salmonid eye is very precise and any failure to connect with a fly is usually deliberate — their eyes are too sharp and so they suspect the artificial for what it is.

FEEDING AND GROWTH

The diet of salmonids is very varied, but it is always food of animal origin. They are obligatory carnivores. Moreover they consume a wide range of insect life, snails, small fishes, worms and even frogs.

The very young fish, newly hatched, will only eat the smallest larval insect forms but as they grow so their appetite changes. It is important to remember, from the point of view of growth, that the larger the fish is, the more energy it will have to expend in chasing a food animal. Consequently from an energy point of view a 4 lb trout is not being very clever if it takes a small fly. Big fish do take small flies and small artificials also, but they can only form a very small part of the total diet as otherwise the fish would wear itself down hunting its food. By the time its weight is around a pound, the trout will have to feed on small fish with worms and frogs in season unless insect life is very rich. By the time it is two or three pounds, small fish will almost certainly make up most of its diet for much of the year although it will still take Mayflies, shrimps and brandling worms as a proportion of its diet, especially in summer.

Salmon and sea-trout at sea feed on a wide variety of marine foods. Crustacean animals must form a reasonable proportion of their diet, as it is from these that they obtain the vitamin A (carotene) responsible for the red colour of their flesh. Salmon on the main oceanic feeding grounds consume a variety of fish and invertebrates such as krill but off the coast of West Greenland, the main feeding ground, they largely consume a small herring-like fish, the capelin. Once it returns to its home river, the salmon does not feed. Indeed it cannot as its gut breaks down and becomes non-functioning. Only when it reaches the well-mended kelt stage does it start to feed again. If this is so, as it indubitably is, why then do they take a worm, or a fly, dangled by the angler, in front of their noses? There is no convincing explanation for this phenomenon, indeed many of the Pacific salmon are impossible to lure onto a hook in freshwater. The only possibility is that they still retain an atavistic urge to snap at something going past their nose, harking back to the hard times of their youth when it was a matter of survival to snap at every moving object, for food.

In a trout lake or river, the diet of the fish varies throughout the year but insects do form a very significant part of the diet of the 'fishable' population, that is the fish between 6 ozs and a pound. These insects may spend their whole life in the water, e.g. the water beetles and water boatmen, or more commonly only spend their young stages in water, as nymphs, which emerge to fly over the water as Mayflies, Stoneflies, midges etc. (*see* Chapter 4). Trout feed on all of these stages and it is these which most of the brown and black fly patterns are dressed to represent. The silver patterns such as the Bloody Butcher, Teal and Silver and Peter Ross, however, almost certainly represent the image of a small fish, or a water beetle with its shiny gas bubble, rather than a fly or its larva, the nymph.

Trout living in waters flowing through mineral-rich soils, especially soils in limestone areas which are rich in calcium, usually grow better than those from peaty hill streams or lochs. This is probably due to the greater availability of food of great variety but the acidity of the water itself (pH), also affects their growth rate. Waters of a low pH, that is acid waters, are usually found in the North and West of the British Isles. Growth rates of trout vary very considerably between waters. Rainbow trout usually grow faster, and in a good limestone area, wild planted rainbows can grow to a pound in just over a year and a half, whereas a brown trout may take three years. In fish farms, where virtually all rainbow trout originate, rainbows which are stuffed with rich pelleted food at every opportunity can grow to 20 lbs in four years but these monsters are really freaks presented to entice the angler, and in the wild, in their native waters, rainbows do not normally approach this size.

PARASITES AND DISEASE

Trout and salmon are final or intermediate hosts to a number of parasites. In the wild these are relatively unimportant but in a densely stocked fishery they may pose problems. The salmon angler is well aware of the salmon louse, a small dark brown, hard parasite which has a round body, and often a pair of long white egg sacs. These are really crustacean animals related to crabs, and are only able to live in the sea. They rapidly fall off the fish and die soon after it reaches fresh water, so they are prized by the salmon angler as indicating that a fish is fresh run from the sea.

The gill maggot is another crustacean parasite which as its name implies lives and feeds on the gills. It does not grow on the gills of young fish but parasitises the gills of adults as they pass through the estuary. Once they attach to the gills they can cause considerable damage and are not affected by the return of a kelt to the sea so that if you catch a fresh run salmon or rarely a sea-trout with gill maggots on it and damaged gills you can be sure that it has spawned at least once before.

Many newly established and densely stocked rainbow trout

reservoir fisheries have been afflicted with a problem of blindness in their fish. Anglers often claim jokingly that all of the fish in a loch are blind but in cases such as this it is in fact true. The reason is that the lenses of their eyes are invaded by a parasite, the eye fluke. This fluke passes to the fish from water snails, and when they invade the lens of the eye they settle there, blinding it and thus making it more liable to capture by the wild birds which are the final host of the fluke.

Much more common are the worms found in the digestive tract, swim bladder and occasionally in cysts in the actual abdominal cavity. These worms are usually white or red and wriggle when the fish is opened up. This causes anglers, or more often their wives, to dispose of the fish rather than cook it. This is completely unnecessary as they are not dangerous, provided they are cooked — indeed they are good nourishing protein.

A more serious disease problem affecting salmon and trout in large numbers in summer and autumn is the disease known as furunculosis. This was so important in the 1930's that Parliament set up the Furunculosis Commission to investigate it. It is caused by a bacterium similar to the typhoid bacillus. It grows in the fish in warm weather and produces large red boils on the skin. Obviously such fish should not be eaten, and when seen they should be removed from the water to limit spread of the infection.

The other disease which has concerned the angling community recently is the disease of salmon and sea-trout known as UDN or Ulcerative Dermal Necrosis. This condition develops as the returning fish enter fresh water and starts off as small ulcers on the head which get infected by fungus spores in the river. The origin of the ulcers is not known but once the fungus has started to grow in them they enlarge and eventually the fungus covers most of the fish. Affected fish can hang around in the river for a long period but ultimately they die. UDN seems to have a seasonal incidence, being much worse in winter and spring. Outbreaks seem to occur every 50 years or so and last for 10 years or more before eventually waning. A great deal of research on the cause of this disease has been carried out but although it seems likely that a virus is responsible for the initial ulceration it has not yet been identified.

Dermot Wilson

The Most Suitable Tackle

The title of this chapter has been advisedly chosen. It is far more important to obtain suitable flyfishing tackle than expensive tackle. Your tackle must be right for the sort of flyfishing you want to do, and that doesn't mean it has to cost a lot.

How do you set about getting the right tackle? First, remember that no rod can be best at everything. (The most suitable rod for distance-casting on reservoirs will not, for instance, be suitable for delicate flyfishing on small streams.) You'll have to make some choices between different sorts of tackle.

Distance or delicacy?
This is probably the most important choice of all. Will you need to cast a long way, even if it means sacrificing presentation (i.e. putting a fly down very accurately, very gently, very delicately)? Or will it be wiser to concentrate on better presentation at shorter distances? The decision will depend to a large extent on the waters you will be fishing and how they will be fished. Fishing from the shores of large still waters such as reservoirs will almost certainly require equipment that enables long-distance casting. It's virtually essential. But fishing overgrown little brooks, to take the opposite extreme, requires accuracy and delicacy, not distance. A long and powerful rod would only be an encumbrance. Between these two extremes are many other types of water, such as small lakes or ponds, and large or medium-size rivers. Each of these requires tackle which provides the right balance between distance and presentation.

All these considerations will be discussed later on. But meanwhile, try to imagine the sort of water you are most likely to fish. It will help to avoid making basic mistakes in the choice of tackle. If you expect to fish several different sorts of water you can always choose 'compromise' tackle — but then you can at least make sure that it isn't unsuitable for the waters you'll be fishing most frequently.

HOW GOOD 'BALANCE' ASSISTS CASTING

The phrase 'balanced tackle' is often heard. What does it mean? 'Balanced tackle' means well-matched tackle — i.e. a set of tackle in which each individual item is well suited to the others. The two items which *must suit* each other are the rod and line.

A rod works in much the same way as an archer's bow — which has to bend before it can shoot an arrow. Similarly, a rod has to flex backwards before it can propel a line forwards. A rod can also be compared with a springboard — which has to be 'loaded' before it can store up or release energy. When casting, the rod is flexed by the weight of the line in the air pulling at the rod-tip. It isn't the angler who flexes the rod, it's the weight of the line.

Rods vary in flexibility. Flylines vary in weight. The weight of the flyline must be just right for the flexibility of the rod. If the flyline is too light, the rod will be underloaded. It will not flex as it should and it will not propel the line. If the line is too heavy, the rod will be overloaded and will not be able to keep the line moving properly through the air If the line is much too heavy it may even strain or break the rod. If on the other hand the weight of the flyline matches the rod correctly, the advantages are two-fold:

(a) The rod will flex properly and will send the line out straight and true.
(b) Casting will soon become a pleasure, as it should be, and will never seem like hard work.

So the partnership of rod and line is absolutely vital. Other aspects of 'balanced tackle' are far less important.

THE FLYLINE — FIRST AND FOREMOST

The whole purpose of the rod is to propel the flyline. Neither rod nor reel can therefore be wisely chosen until the type and weight of the flyline have been settled. Everything starts with the line — and in particular with its weight.

The Importance of Weight

Unlike spinning lines or coarse-fishing lines, flylines are purposely made to have weight so that they can bend a flyrod. The various weights of line are classified according to AFTM numbers. (AFTM stands for the Association of Fishing Tackle Manufacturers, which devised the classification.) The various numbers denote the relative weights of the first 30 ft of flyline — plus any level tip. The AFTM scale goes from 1 to 12, each successive number indicating a heavier line. The phrase 'AFTM No.' is usually shown as the symbol #. So if you see #6 on a flyline-box the line inside will be an AFTM No. 6 line.

Light lines (#3 to #5) can only be used with a flexible rod that is neither stiff nor very powerful. Used with such rods, light lines have certain advantages. They land gently on the water and are not likely to frighten the fish by making a splash. They cast less shadow, because they are thinner than heavier lines. Thus they are excellent for difficult conditions such as clear, calm, low water or bright sunshine. And they are particularly useful for shy trout.

Light lines can and should be used whenever you don't have to cast a long way or into a strong wind. They are ideal on small streams or medium-sized rivers like the Hampshire chalk-streams. They are occasionally useful on still waters as well — for instance, when fishing calm water near the shore, or fishing downwind from a boat.

Heavy lines (#8 to #10) can and should be used with a stiff-ish and more powerful rod. (A less powerful rod would not be able to handle the weight of the line.) Heavy lines have advantages which are quite different from those of light lines. Their weight adds to their momentum when casting, helping them to travel a long way and to overcome air- and wind-resistance. Heavy lines are therefore preferable to light lines whenever distance is more important than perfect presentation. (In a particularly tricky wind, it is also a good idea to use a line one size heavier than usual.) For instance, on large still waters heavy lines or fairly heavy lines are advisable. Here the *capacity* to cast a long way is essential, even though it may be possible to catch plenty of fish at shorter range as well. Perfect presentation (especially when there's a ripple or wave on the water) is less vital. Even with a heavy-ish line, however, presentation can with practice be fairly good. #11 and #12 lines are for big salmon rods.

Medium-weight lines (#6 and #7) are the workaday general-purpose lines used by most fishermen. They cast farther than light-weight lines and perform a little better in wind, though they do not touch down on the water quite so lightly or delicately. Nevertheless, they present a fly perfectly well enough in most circumstances. A #6 line, for instance, is the weight most commonly used for dry-fly fishing on rivers, where considerable delicacy is needed.

Although medium-weight lines are less easy than heavier lines to cast a long way, they will achieve sufficient distance for almost any river, and for small still waters as well. Because of the superior presentation they allow, they are better than heavy lines for ponds and small lakes — though heavier lines are needed on big reservoirs. Used with rods of average flexibility they are ideal for all-purpose flyfishing — with the single exception of reservoirs and large still waters.

Floating or Sinking?

During recent decades great advances have been made in the design and manufacture of flylines. Each line consists of a core surrounded by a plastic 'dressing' and it is the density of the latter (i.e. whether it's denser or less dense than water) which determines whether a line floats or sinks. Furthermore, different sinking lines can have dressings of different densities which lead them to sink at differing speeds. Thus there are 'extra-fast-sinking lines' (with the most dense dressing), 'fast-sinking lines' and 'slow-sinking lines'. The denser the dressing of a flyline of a given weight, the thinner it will be. Four different #6 lines, for instance, would have identical weights but they would have different diameters if they happened to be, say, floating, slow-sinking, fast-sinking and extra-fast-sinking lines. The floating line would be the thickest.

When should you use a floating line, and when a sinking line? Obviously, dry-fly fishing demands a floating line. Not quite so obviously, so does a great deal of wet-fly and nymph fishing. When a wet fly or nymph is used with a floating line, its weight draws some or all of the leader — the length of nylon between line-tip and fly — beneath the surface. The heavier the fly and the slower the current, the more nylon will be taken down — and the last foot or so of the line may also be drawn under. Theoretically, if you're fishing still water with a floating line and a fairly heavy wet fly or nymph, you can fish as deep as your leader is long. Normally, however, the process of retrieving the line raises the fly more towards the surface. But even so, lengthening the leader is a good way of fishing a little deeper than usual.

Floating lines, then, should be used for fishing on or near the surface. Their uses include:

(a) All dry-fly fishing on both still and running water.
(b) Wet-fly fishing for trout on almost all rivers. Fish which are ready to take will be 'up in the water' and a floating line normally gets flies deep enough.
(c) Most wet-fly fishing for sea-trout, whether by day or night, in any kind of water. Some sea-trout are caught on sinking lines, but far fewer than are caught on floating lines.

(d) Most flyfishing for salmon, particularly in summer when the water is comparatively warm. In early spring and autumn a sinking line may be better, since salmon take deep when the water is cold.

(e) Wet-fly or nymph fishing for stillwater trout with many of the 'imitative' (as opposed to 'attractor') patterns of fly. These are often most effective when fished fairly close to the surface and retrieved very slowly.

A further advantage of a floating line is the ease with which it can be 'picked up' from the surface for re-casting. This makes it an excellent line for beginners. A sinking line needs more practice before it can be handled well. Sinking lines are, however, essential as an alternative on nearly all still waters. Many stillwater fishermen catch more trout on them than on floating lines. They are virtually obligatory for the following purposes:

(a) Fast, deep retrieving in still water. This is often carried out with large wet flies called 'lures', and for these a fast-sinking or extra-fast-sinking line is usually vital.

(b) Fishing really deep in still water even when retrieving *slowly*. Again a fast-sinking or extra-fast-sinking line will be necessary — because even these take far longer to reach the depths than most people imagine.

(c) Fishing fairly close to the surface in still water — whenever you're retrieving at a speed faster than 'very slow'. (A floating line, unless retrieved *very* slowly, brings the fly to the surface.) For this situation a slow-sinking line is often best.

(d) Flyfishing for salmon when the water is cold. Then a fast-sinking line and a comparatively large, heavy fly will usually be called for.

One other type of line should be mentioned. It is called a 'sink-tip' line — and is in fact a floating line except for its tip, which consists of several yards of sinking line. It is not one of the most commonly used lines, but it can be very handy in certain circumstances:

(a) Salmon fishermen find it useful whenever and wherever the current might make a fly skate along the surface if fished on a floating line — e.g. the glide at the tail of a pool. Then a sink-tip line keeps the fly swimming where it should be — just below the surface.

(b) Stillwater trout fishermen (and a few river fishermen)

occasionally use it too — when they need a line that fishes a fly slightly deeper than a floating line but not so deep as a sinking line.

Drift-fishing from a boat (*see* p. 110) is usually practised with a floating line. If the boat is anchored, however, the same range of lines can be used as from the shore.

Many river fishermen never need any line other than a floating line. But a stillwater fisherman needs to be able to vary the depth at which he fishes — and also the speed at which he retrieves. One floating line and one sinking line, at the very least, should accompany him on his fishing trips. Serious and successful stillwater fishermen often carry more lines — 3, 4 or even 5 — to suit different conditions and different fishing techniques. They would feel unbearably handicapped if they did not allow themselves this degree of versatility. Their choice of line will frequently be more important to them than their choice of rod.

Which Sort of Taper?

All good flylines taper. They are designed so that there is a comparatively thick part near the tip-ring of the rod which helps in providing weight to flex the rod itself. They then taper down to a fine tip — which allows for delicacy and a smooth transmission of impetus from rod-tip to line-tip. Level or untapered lines, which can still be obtained, don't perform nearly so well.

There are four main varieties of taper — double-taper, forward-taper (also called weight-forward), shooting head, and finally single-taper (often called a half-line). The first two of these are 'full lines' — usually 30 yards long, sometimes up to 40. The standard shooting head is only 10 yards in length, while a single-taper line is a 'half-line' and is therefore normally 15 yards long. The profiles of these various tapers are shown diagrammatically in figure 3.

Each taper behaves in a different way and has a different purpose. One of the main differences lies in the amount of line you can 'shoot' (*see* p. 50). The extra distance gained by shooting depends largely on the taper of the line.

Double-taper lines are the most popular type. They have certain advantages and disadvantages:

(*a*) Since the two halves of a double-taper line are identical, it has two usable ends. When one end begins to wear out, you can simply reverse the line on the reel and use the other end. Thus each line has a double life.

(*b*) They are easy to cast, because however much line is aerialised there is always thick line at the rod-tip. (This is important for good casting and less easy to judge with a forward-taper line — see below.) For the same reason, a double-taper line turns over smoothly in the air — and this helps good presentation.

(*c*) So far, so good. But double-taper lines are not particularly efficient for long-distance casting, because the friction of the thick line in the rod-rings inhibits easy shooting.

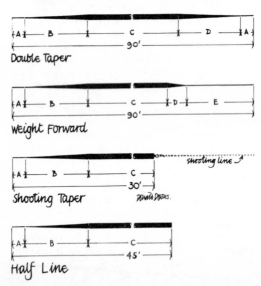

3. *Line tapers. A* = LEVEL LINE-TIP: *2 ft long. B* = FRONT TAPER: *8—10 ft. C* = BELLY: *65—70 ft for double-taper lines, 14—30 ft for forward-taper lines, according to 'lift' required. D* = REAR TAPER: *same as front taper for double-taper lines, 3—8 ft for forward-taper lines. E* = RUNNING LINE: *used only for 'shooting'*

Forward-taper lines are similar to double-taper lines so far as the part that you aerialise is concerned — i.e. the first dozen yards or so. But then, instead of a long thick 'belly' and a reverse taper at the other end, the rest of a forward-taper line consists of thin 'running line' (*see* figure 3). Here are the characteristics of forward-taper lines:

(a) You can shoot far more forward-taper line than double-taper line because the thin running line slips more easily through the rod-rings than the thicker belly of the double-taper. Greater distance is therefore possible. But too much forward-taper line should never be aerialised — because if there is more than about a yard of running line beyond the rod-tip it becomes very difficult to control the line in the air. Distance should be gained by shooting, not by aerialisation.

(b) Although the front taper of a forward-taper line is very similar to that of a double-taper line, it is not entirely identical. The weight is distributed just a little more towards the front. One effect of this is to make the line turn over a little better into a wind, though perhaps only marginally so.

(c) Because so much of a forward-taper line consists of thin running line, the whole flyline is less bulky than a double-taper line and therefore fits on a smaller and lighter reel. Alternatively you can have more 'backing' on your reel. (Backing is the thin braided or monofilament line which is attached to the rear end of the flyline, allowing a powerful fish to take out extra line if it wishes.)

Shooting heads, as their name implies, are designed to allow maximum distances to be shot. A standard ready-made head consists of only 10 yards or so of flyline — the equivalent of the first 10 yards of a full line. At the rear end is a loop which is attached to monofilament backing. When casting you first of all aerialise the 'head', plus a yard or two at most of the monofilament backing. Then you shoot more backing for distance, the monofilament running through the rod-rings with even greater ease than the running line of a forward-taper line.

A shooting head needs a certain amount of practice to be handled well. The abrupt change in diameter from monofilament to flyline makes it more difficult to achieve smooth turn-over and good presentation. In addition, some fishermen prefer the feel of ordinary flyline to the feel of monofilament in their left hands. With these provisos, however, a shooting head is an extremely efficient type of line for distance-casting and is the favourite of many reservoir fishermen. It takes up even less room on a spool than does a forward-taper line, permitting a very small, light reel and ample backing.

The idea of the loop at the butt-end of a ready-made shooting head is to allow a quick change to a heavier or lighter head. Most fishermen, however, only use one head on any single reel or spare spool. A smoother join can then be made by cutting off the loop and needle-knotting (*see* figure 4) the monofilament to the rear end of the shooting head.

Single-taper lines — commonly called half-lines — are quite widely used these days. They consist of half a double-taper line and therefore only cost about half as much. Furthermore, they have certain advantages:

(*a*) They provide quite enough flyline for most purposes — 45 ft of line plus 9 ft of leader, plus say 9 ft of rod, is ample for casts of about 20 yards.

(*b*) Half-lines are obviously less bulky than full lines, and allow small, light reels to be used.

(*c*) They can easily be made into home-made shooting heads. This is the type that many good flyfishermen prefer, since they may wish to aerialise rather more than the 10 yards of a standard head. Fifteen yards is usually too much, however, so they often snip off about three yards from the back of the half-line to leave themselves with a 12-yard shooting head, which they then needle-knot to monofilament backing.

If you make up a shooting head in this way, remember that the AFTM No. of any line is based on the weight of the first 30 ft (plus the level tip). If you aerialise more than 30 ft, you are in effect loading the rod with a higher AFTM No. As a rough guide, each extra 6 ft adds one AFTM No. A 12-yard shooting head made from #7 line will therefore weigh as much as a standard 10-yard #8 shooting head, and will be suitable for a rod that casts best with #8 line.

The Colour of Flylines
We cannot be sure what a flyline looks like to a fish. Underwater photographs have been taken — and observers have often sunk themselves below the surface to look up at flylines — but we cannot assume that a fish sees things as we do. Nevertheless, we can probably take it for granted that a flyline is least visible to a fish when it corresponds in tone (rather than colour) to the background against which it will be seen. Here are some guidelines:

(*a*) A floating line is often seen by fish against the background of the sky. It will therefore be least conspicuous if it is light in tone. White and light orange are two useful colours. In many circumstances, however, the colour of a floating line is not very important. A shy trout may be frightened by line of any colour, so it is best not to let him see it all. Apart from the fly, only the leader should be in his vision.

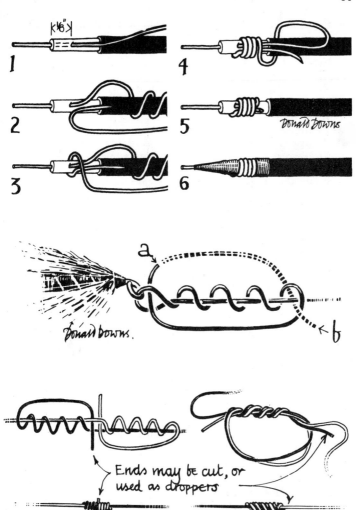

4. *Some essential knots.* (Top) *needle knot for attaching leader butt to line. (Illustrated with line dressing stripped — but this is not essential.)* (Centre) *Blood knot for attaching fly to leader-tip. Cut at a or tucked at b for additional security.* (Bottom) *Knots for joining together lengths of nylon — the double blood knot* (left) *and the water knot. Particularly useful for making droppers*

(b) On some waters, such as those bordered by tall trees, a floating line is more likely to be seen against foliage. Then a darker colour, such as green or brown, may be preferable. It may also be better for wet-fly fishing with a floating line or sink-tip line.

(c) Sinking lines are normally seen against a dark background and are therefore fairly dark in tone — either green or brown.

Manufacturers' Markings

All flylines are described by a combination of letters and numbers which appear on the box and are used in catalogues. These markings are made up of three components which describe the type of taper, the AFTM No. and the floating/sinking properties of the line. The abbreviations and the order in which they are used are shown below:

DT = double-taper		F = floating
WF = weight-forward, i.e. forward-taper	AFTM No.	S = sinking
ST = shooting-taper, i.e. shooting head.		F/S = float/sink,
Also, though rarely, single-taper		i.e. sink-tip

For example, a DT—6—F line is a #6 double-taper floating line, an ST—8—S line is a #8 shooting head made of sinking line and a WF—7—F/S is a #7 forward-taper sink-tip line.

CHOOSING A TROUT ROD

As we've already seen, the weight of flyline should dictate the flexibility of the rod. All modern flyrods have the weight of line for which they were designed marked on the butt just above the handle.

The Right Length

For convenience let us describe any rod longer than 9 ft as 'long', any rod from 8 to 9 ft as 'medium-length' and any rod under 8 ft as 'short'. All have their uses.

Long rods:

(a) They are at their most effective on reservoirs and other large still waters, where distance is usually more important than perfect presentation.

(b) For distance-casting, they should be powerful enough to handle a fairly heavy line (about #8) provided always that the rod is not so heavy or so stiff that it's tiring to use. These characteristics in turn depend to some extent on the material from which the rod is made (*see* p. 35). For instance, any single-handed cane rod longer than 9 ft is liable to tire the average fisherman. This is one reason why cane rods are not in common use among stillwater fishermen. Fibreglass is considerably lighter — a 9¼ ft glass rod weighing about 5 oz can be first-class for still water. Some stillwater fishermen can even use a 10 ft glass rod. Carbon fibre is the lightest rod-making material of all — a 9½ or 10 ft rod can weigh 4 oz and can be very easily handled. Even longer carbon-fibre rods are perfectly practicable — but weight isn't everything. The extra leverage exerted on the wrist by a very long rod should also be borne in mind.

(c) A fairly long rod is always useful when 'drift fishing' from a boat with a 'team' of wet flies. Trout often take the 'top dropper' (the fly nearest the rod-tip) as you retrieve it and bring it skipping along the surface of the water. Since this is done by raising the rod-tip, a long rod is useful.

A medium-length rod (8 to 9 ft) is an ideal all-purpose rod for smaller still waters and for nearly all rivers other than little brooks and streams. Here are some comments:

(a) A 9 ft rod is a very good all-rounder, capable of adequate distance for large still waters and perfect for smaller still waters. Furthermore, it is not too long or cumbersome for most rivers. A 9 ft single-handed cane rod may be a little on the heavy side, but not for those who particularly like cane. A 9 ft glass- or carbon-fibre rod will be light enough for anyone except perhaps a child.

(b) Rods from 8 to 8¾ ft are primarily river-fishing rods and are perfect for this purpose. Whichever material they're made of, they are light enough to handle easily and present any sort of trout fly exceptionally well. A river fisherman should choose a rod-length which suits the size of stream he fishes — 8 to 8½ ft is long enough for many medium-sized streams. Remember, presentation is more important than distance on almost any river.

(c) 8 or 8½ ft is a good length for any young fisherman from about the age of 7. If it's made of fibreglass it won't be too heavy for him or her and can cost very little. It is a mistake to give a youngster a 'miniature' rod of under 8 ft because he'll find it more difficult to keep his backcast well up behind him.

A short flyrod (under 8 ft and occasionally no more than 6 ft) is extremely useful for brook fishing. Also, it can give great pleasure to anyone fishing a wider stream who enjoys using a small, delicate rod with as light a line as possible. Like other lengths of rod, it has its advantages and disadvantages:

(a) On a very overgrown little brook a short rod allows you to cast in and among bushes and trees.

(b) Even if it's made of cane (the heaviest rod-making material) it will still be very light and very pleasant to use.

(c) Although short rods can be made stiff enough to throw fairly heavy lines, they are also ideal for light lines (#4, or even #3) and thus for very delicate fishing.

(d) Short rods need practice to handle well because there is 'less rod' to do the work. They also make it a little harder to keep the backcast up in the air. Beginners are therefore wise to start with a rod of 8 ft or longer.

(e) When playing a fish, you have less control with a short rod than with a longer one. For instance, it's less easy to keep a trout away from weeds.

Which Material?

Each of the three materials from which flyrods are built — cane, fibreglass and carbon fibre — has its staunch supporters. But the truth is that excellent flyrods can be made from any of the three materials. (So can some appallingly bad ones!) Nevertheless, the materials do have different properties which to some extent affect their suitability for different sorts of flyrod, though the differences should not be exaggerated.

The table opposite summarises the most important features of each material.

Weight is a factor which militates against the use of cane in trout rods of over 9 ft. Longer rods are best made in fibreglass or carbon fibre.

'Speed of action' refers to the way in which the materials bend and unbend. Cane is leisurely in this respect — the line sails out over the water in a characteristically smooth and unhurried way, and this assists delicate casting and good presentation. The faster actions of fibreglass and carbon fibre enable the line to be cast at a higher velocity and in a narrower loop (*see* figure 5). This facilitates distance-casting. In addition, it's of some assistance when you're casting into a wind. Casting close-at-hand or with light lines is easier with cane or carbon-fibre rods than with glass rods, since glass rods need rather more 'pull' at the rod-tip before flexing properly.

In terms of cost, carbon fibre is the most expensive material and fibreglass the cheapest. Fibreglass is perfectly adequate for most purposes, however, and is excellent for long rods such as those used for fishing reservoirs or drift-fishing. Cane rods are more expensive than glass rods, mainly because they're built by craftsmen rather than being mass-produced. They have a unique 'feel' which makes them loved and treasured by many flyfishermen on rivers. (Don't believe the tales you hear about cane being old-fashioned. It's a marvellous rod-building material, especially for medium-length and short rods.) Carbon-fibre rods are very expensive and are even lighter and faster than glass rods. They are also much thinner than glass rods, particularly at the butt, which gives them a pleasing appearance and cuts down on the air-resistance caused by moving a rod backwards and forwards. Many fishermen, however, simply do not *need* the particular advantages of carbon fibre — and can save money by choosing a glass rod instead.

PROPERTIES AND USES OF ROD-MAKING MATERIALS

Material	Weight of typical 8'6" flyrod	Cost	Speed of action	Ideal applications
Cane (called bamboo in U.S.A.)	4¾ oz	Fairly expensive	Slow	River & brook fishing. Casting close-at-hand. Light lines. Good presentation.
Fibreglass	3¾ oz	Inexpensive	Fairly fast	All situations, but particularly distance-casting and drift-fishing on still water.
Carbon fibre (called graphite in U.S.A.)	2¾ oz	Very expensive	Very fast	All situations again — including use of light lines. Possesses advantages of glass in greater degree.

Salmon and Sea-trout Rods

Flyrods for salmon are naturally more powerful than trout rods. Most of them are considerably longer too, and therefore designed

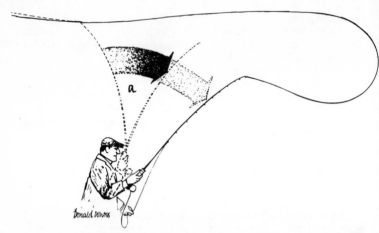

5. *A rod which describes a 'wide arc' (a, above) will throw a 'wide loop', whereas a rod which describes a 'narrow arc' (b, right) will throw a narrow loop. A narrow loop is far better for distance-casting, accuracy and the overcoming of air resistance*

for double-handed casting. The extra length of a salmon rod is not only for the handling of heavier fish, but also to allow the fly to be fished more effectively. By enabling the line to be held out over tricky currents it helps the fisherman to let the fly swim exactly where he wishes (and at the right speed). Also, of course, it assists distance-casting on broad rivers.

The right length and power for a salmon rod will depend on the size of the salmon, the size of the river and the size of the fly — the colder the water, the larger the fly used. A fairly long and powerful rod of 14 or even 15 ft is suitable for big rivers and heavy coldwater flies. A smaller rod of 12 ft or so is suitable for narrower rivers and lighter summer flies. A rather more powerful rod is advisable for a sinking line than for a floating line, since more strain is put on the rod each time the line is retrieved from beneath the surface for recasting. A rod of about 13 ft, capable of handling a #9 line, makes a good all-round double-handed salmon rod. Smaller salmon rods will handle #8 lines, while larger ones may need lines up to #11 or #12.

Single-handed rods (from 9 to 10 ft) are also perfectly suitable on many rivers in summer conditions, when fairly light flies are being used. They are excellent for drift fishing on lochs as well. Such a rod will usually handle a #7 or #8 line.

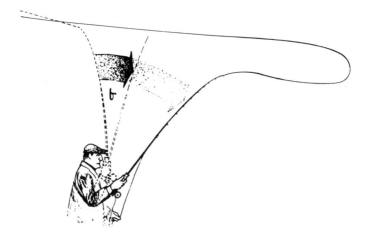

The choice of material for a salmon rod is often dictated by purely personal preference, and by price as well. The extra weight of cane is a less significant factor in double-handed rods than in single-handed ones, but cane's aptitude for good presentation is less important for salmon than for trout. A good fibreglass salmon rod will perform very well and be considerably less expensive than a cane or a carbon-fibre rod.

A suitable rod for sea-trout need not be very different from an ordinary trout rod. Often the same rod will serve both purposes. A medium-length trout rod can be excellent for average-sized sea-trout in fairly small rivers. For larger sea-trout in larger rivers (or for drift fishing) the ideal rod would perhaps be 9 or 10 ft, designed for a #7 line. But a good reservoir rod makes a serviceable alternative and can often be used for light salmon as well.

CHOOSING A FLYREEL

The choice of flyreel is a less vital matter than the choice of rod and line. Provided the reel is not altogether too heavy, it will have very little influence on casting performance. The main task of a flyreel is to store the flyline and backing in a convenient way. Obviously it should be reliable — most modern flyreels are — but it need not be either elaborate or expensive. A simple flyreel, which turns the drum once for each turn of the handle, is usually quite suitable. There are two main types:

(a) The traditional type, in which the spool revolves inside the cage. An adjustable 'check' or 'drag' is desirable to allow you to vary the degree of pull needed before the reel gives out line. Choose this according to the strength of your tackle and the size of fish you expect.

(b) The 'rim control' type, in which the spool has a flange which revolves on the outside of the reel. This allows a running fish to be braked by lightly touching the rim while it's turning. An adjustable check can then be dispensed with, though it's often included as a useful extra.

Then there are two types of less simple reel:

(a) The multiplying reel has a gearing system which leads the drum to revolve more than once with each turn of the handle. The precise ratio varies with different reels but is normally in the region of 2—to—1.

(b) The automatic flyreel has a mechanism (usually clockwork) which does away with the necessity for any reel-handle at all. When a lever is depressed, the drum revolves automatically and winds line back onto the reel.

These reels both have the virtue of retrieving line far more rapidly than simple reels do. A good many fishermen find this a worthwhile and significant asset. Others, however, believe that the simple reel gives them more control over a hooked fish than does the clockwork machinery of an automatic reel, and that it's easier and less stiff to turn than most multiplying reels. The choice is entirely a matter of personal preference. It's true that multiplying

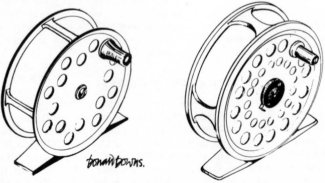

6. (Above) *the traditional type of reel* (left) *and the 'rim control' type.* (Top right) *cross sections through rims*

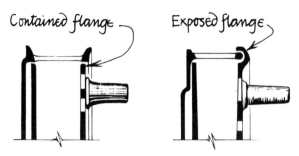

reels are just a little heavier than simple reels and that automatic reels are heavier still. They both also cost a little more, but they suit some fishermen very well indeed.

It used to be said that the weight of a flyreel should 'balance the rod'. This is largely an old wives' tale, because there is no ideal 'point of balance'. Most rods would indeed cast best with no reel at all. The only case in which balance is important is when there is a good deal of weight beyond your hand, such as with a 9½ ft cane rod. Then a fairly heavy reel acts as a counter-balance and prevents the rod from feeling top-heavy. In other circumstances, it's sensible to have a fairly light reel.

All modern flyreels have quick-release spools, so if you want to carry more than one line (as stillwater fishermen usually do) there's no need to have more than one reel. You can use spare spools instead.

There's one other important point to make about flyreels. The reel you choose must obviously be able to hold your flyline and a sufficient quantity of backing. In other words, it must be the right size. This makes it all the more logical to choose your line or lines before choosing your reel. The capacities of all reels are stated by the manufacturers in their catalogues and advertisements, and sometimes on the reel boxes. These stated capacities are *sometimes* a little optimistic, so ask your tackle dealer to wind your line and backing onto the reel. Here are some other factors to bear in mind:

(a) A double-taper floating line requires more room than any other sort of line. For instance, if your reel holds a DT—6—F line with a given amount of backing, it will hold any other #6 flyline with more backing.

(b) Sinking lines take up less room than floating lines because they're thinner. Forward-taper lines take up less room than double-taper lines, and shooting heads or half-lines take up less room still.

(c) The required amount of backing depends on your type of fishing. On many rivers, especially small rivers, trout do not run far, so little or no backing is needed. Large open waters are a different matter, particularly if they hold large fish. At least 40 or 50 yards of backing will be necessary. And for salmon fishing on large waters you may well need 100 yards of backing.

(d) Make sure that the spool of the reel is 'bulked up' with sufficient backing so that the end of the flyline is about ¼"below the rim. If the spool is insufficiently filled, each revolution of the drum will take in very little line.

LEADERS

Of all the items of tackle that a flyfisherman uses, the leader or cast is perhaps the one that is most frequently neglected. Yet the composition and taper of a leader are vital to good casting and good presentation. In all circumstnces which call for reasonable presentation, your leader should be just as carefully tapered as your flyline. Otherwise, however well you cast the flyline, your leader may fail to straighten out properly — especially against a wind. You are likely to find it falling in a sad and sorry little heap around your line-tip.

A frequent shortcoming of shop-bought leaders (as opposed to home-made leaders) is that many of them have butts which are not thick enough. To continue the taper of the flyline into the leader, and to allow energy to flow without interruption from rod-tip to fly, the nylon at the leader-butt should have a diameter of at least 0.45 mm — i.e. 20—25 lb breaking strain.

Another barrier to good presentation, though rather less important, is an over-bulky line-to-leader knot. The common figure-of-eight knot, for instance, is certainly on the bulky side. Learn to tie a kneedle-knot (*see* figure 4) if you can, because it makes the smoothest possible join between flyline and leader. Failing that, use one of the plastic cast connectors which are available in the shops.

The diameter of your leader-tip will probably be governed by several considerations. Large fish obviously warrant thicker and stronger leader-tips than small fish. Wary and 'well-educated' fish can often only be caught on comparatively fine leader-tips. Very bright weather or low, clear water may also call for a fine leader-tip. The size of fly is also important. A small fly behaves unnaturally if it's tied to a thick leader-tip. Equally, with a fine leader-tip it is difficult to turn over a large bushy fly such as a Mayfly against a contrary breeze. Leader-tips can be classified, perhaps rather arbitrarily, as shown in the table below. Fine and medium leader-tips are suitable for river trout. Strong tips are useful for large reservoir fish and sea-trout, while extra-strong tips are for salmon.

LEADER-TIP DIAMETERS (mm)

Fine (5X and 4X)	0.16—0.18
Medium (3X)	0.20
Strong (2X and 1X)	0.22—0.24
Extra Strong	0.28—0.35

Home-made leaders (the most economic) are made up by knotting together a number of lengths of nylon, stepping down the diameter at each knot. Here are some points to remember:

(a) Each step should reduce the diameter of the nylon by no more than 0.05 mm. Otherwise the leader will be liable to break at the knot. Use blood knots with no fewer than four turns on each side. One other good knot for tying leaders is the water knot. It is very strong but rather bulky, and this makes it most suitable for joining *fine* lengths of nylon together.

(b) The first length of nylon, which forms the butt of the leader, should be a long one — almost half the total leader. This long, level butt helps the leader to turn over smoothly. Many good fishermen keep a 4 or 5 ft length of fairly thick nylon (0.45 or 0.50 mm) permanently needle-knotted to the tips of their flylines. When they wish to renew their leaders, they do so only from the end of this permanent butt. It's a good idea.

There are two types of ready-made leader — knotless and knotted. 'Knotless' or 'continuous taper' leaders taper steadily from butt to tip, much as a flyline does. For really good presentation, however, the knotted type of leader is preferable. Its long thick butt, and the slight additional weight of the knots themselves, help it to carry into the wind and straighten out well. It's usually the best type for flyfishing on rivers. But in calm conditions on still water the knots may create little wakes behind them as you retrieve. In circumstances like these there is a good argument for using knotless leaders.

How long should the leader be? The normal length is 9 ft and this will usually serve you well. Longer leaders — up to perhaps 20 ft — can also be effective for certain purposes, sometimes to avoid scaring fish, sometimes to gain a little extra depth when fished with a floating line. But long leaders do need a good deal of skill to handle, especially in a wind. It's seldom if ever desirable, however, to have a leader *shorter* than 9 ft. (Even if you have a shorter rod, the join between line and leader won't catch in the tip-ring if you've used a needle-knot.)

ALL THE REST

There are of course a myriad other items of fishing tackle which you can buy. But in this chapter I've felt it best to deal with the essential items in some depth, rather than giving a more superficial description of all the luxuries and impedimenta which are such a temptation for all fishermen. There's one other essential item, of course — and that's a good selection of flies. Chapters 4 and 5 deal in detail with this aspect of tackle. The list of further necessities isn't very long. It will probably include:

(a) *A landing net.* A net with a rigid frame — either round or oval — is the simplest and most efficient in use. Nets with collapsible triangular frames tend to let you down by getting in a tangle when you need them most. But they do have the advantage of being more compact to pack or carry around. For salmon fishing, you may need a gaff or tailer.

(b) A pair of *thigh-waders* — or perhaps chest-waders if you fish for salmon in large rivers. Cleated rubber soles are adequate for most still waters, and also for rivers with a silt or gravel bed. But for the sake of safety choose felt or studded soles if you are wading in fast rocky streams.

(c) If you're shooting line for distance, you may find a *line-tray* so useful as to be almost essential. It gives you somewhere to coil the line as you retrieve, so that it's ready for trouble-free shooting.

(d) If you use a dry fly, you will need some good *floatant* to make sure that the fly stays buoyant. There are a great many brands — so seek the advice of a good tackle dealer.

And that's that. Almost everything else is either non-essential or extremely easy to improvise. A flybox, for instance, is very useful for keeping flies in — but you can make one from any suitable container by lining it with foam rubber. A fishing bag is useful too — but an old haversack will serve instead.

You may well end up, like most of us, with too much tackle. But there's no need to *start* with too much.

CAUTIONARY FOOTNOTE

Good tackle isn't any substitute at all for skill or knowledge or experience. The right tackle helps a little, but that's all. Fish don't get caught by tackle. They get caught by fishermen.

Philip Tallents

Casting

'The foundation of all good casting is in the mind' wrote Eric Taverner. What he meant was that, like riding a bicycle, skating or ski-ing, fly casting has to be learned, for the movements are not instinctive ones, and the mind must play a dominant part in any activity which does not come naturally.

However, like these other activities, once learnt, casting is rarely completely forgotten, although sloppy practices may develop and reduce one's effectiveness.

Casting is more cerebral than muscular because the tool being used is not a simple stick or stone. It is a carefully designed device for launching a three-stage projectile. The rod is a lever—spring, designed to give the desired impulse to the projectile, of which the first stage is the flyline, the second the leader and the third the fly, which is the payload.

It is difficult to throw away a fly. However hard you try, it will not land far from your feet! Tied to the end of a leader, the result is little better. But it is the first stage of the projectile, the flyline, which has to provide most of the mass and momentum needed to carry the two other stages to their destination. The engineering principle which lies behind this action requires that the line should be tapered, the taper permitting energy to be transmitted smoothly and effectively from line to leader.

The leader itself must of necessity be transparent and very light, and is almost universally made of nylon. It also has to be tapered and sufficiently stiff to transfer the energy given to it by the tip of the line on to the fly. Then the fly can be made to finish its journey, hovering, all energy spent, above the point on the water where the fisherman requires it to fall.

Single-handed fly rods vary in length from about 5 to 10 ft. In their function, as levers, they extend man's arm. A small movement of the fisherman's hand produces a substantial movement of the rod-tip. The rod should be tapered, because that reduces its weight very much and does not impair its function as a lever. More importantly, it is tapered because that makes it more effective as a spring.

A spring is a potential reservoir of energy and that is just what a rod is. When it bends under load it stores energy, releasing that energy when it straightens. It stores energy, put into it by the fisherman's arm, over a relatively long interval of time (perhaps a second). It can be made to release that energy, into the line, in a way that will be most effective in projecting it.

Good technique in casting depends on good timing, which enables energy to be put into the rod and transmitted to the line most effectively. Good technique also allows maximum accuracy in fly presentation and enables the fisherman to achieve the required distance with the minimum amount of effort. If these simple mechanical ideas are fully appreciated, I believe that casting is more easily understood and far more easily learned.

If you have watched a world famous skater or a renowned athlete in action, I expect that some of the following thoughts have passed through your mind. What perfect timing! How beautifully balanced he is! How relaxed he is! How easy he makes it look! What style he has!

Should you see the perspiration pouring off his brow, it will come as quite an ugly surprise. Good fly casting is like that too, except that there is no perspiration. The satisfaction is in doing it right, in the physical ease of doing it well and in the rhythm of well-timed muscular co-ordination — the marrying of sight, touch and movement to ensure that the rod is made to do the utmost amount of work it can possibly do, while the fisherman achieves his objective with the least work.

Let us look at a world-class caster and remember that competitive casting is judged as much for accuracy as for distance. The silhouettes which illustrate this chapter are of world casting champion, Jack Martin, drawn from a series of about 100 photographs which I have taken of him. In all that follows it is assumed that you are right-handed. If you are not, please read right for left and left for right throughout.

THE OVERHEAD CAST

Jack is standing very relaxed, with his right foot just a little forward and his weight a little heavier on that foot than on the left one. He is holding the cork handle of the rod, lying across the middle finger and the two smaller fingers of his right hand. His index finger, though touching the rod, is taking no weight at all. His thumb is lying on top of the rod and pointing forward. He is 'shaking hands' with the rod and holding the cork almost as far forward as is

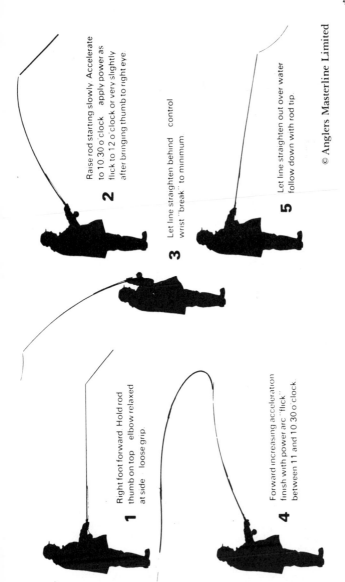

1 Right foot forward Hold rod thumb on top   elbow relaxed at side   loose grip.

2 Raise rod starting slowly Accelerate to 10 30 o'clock   apply power as flick to 12 o'clock or very slightly after bringing thumb to right eye

3 Let line straighten behind   control wrist "break" to minimum

4 Forward increasing acceleration finish with power arc "flick" between 11 and 10 30 o'clock.

5 Let line straighten out over water follow down with rod tip

© Anglers Masterline Limited

7. The overhead cast

possible. The remainder of the butt of the rod is lying under and along his forearm. The rod is balanced in his hand. The length of its stem is counterbalanced by the weight of the reel.

The rod-tip is pointing at the fly, which is on the water at least 20 ft in front of him. The line and leader are stretched between the rod-tip and the fly with no loose coils. Jack's elbow is relaxed by his side and his wrist is straight. His grip is no tighter than is required to hold the rod. Because he is practicing, he has removed the point and barb from the fly and he is also holding the line between his right index finger and the rod butt.

Commencing the back cast, he raises his forearm, using his elbow as a fulcrum. The movement continues until his thumb is just in front of his right eye. That sounds simple enough and indeed it is, but let us look closely at exactly what he did within that simple movement. He started very slowly. As the load of the line came onto the rod-tip and began to bend it, he accelerated his movement. At a point when, if he had looked at his hand and forearm, it had reached about 10 o'clock, he really piled on energy and speed. This had the result that he not only increased the speed of the rod-tip but also made the rod bend very much more. This 'flick' or 'power arc' lasted until his thumb came within 3 or 4 inches of his right eye and there stopped.

Let us analyse why he did that. First of all, he started slowly so that he could get any stretch or loops out of the line before he applied energy to it. You cannot put tension into a slack line or transmit energy through it, any more than you can lean on a rope! He knew he had achieved this tension when the rod began to bend. He knew, therefore, all was now ready for him to apply power to it. There was, already, quite a lot of energy in the bent rod. This stored energy was to be added to further energy that he now began to generate by physical effort up to the point where he stopped his movement. All this energy then poured into the line as the bent rod recovered and straightened.

He brought his thumb up to his right eye because he uses it like a gunsight to fix on the point where he wants the fly to drop.

He kept his wrist unbent because he wants the longest possible lever and he added the length of his wrist and forearm to the length of the rod. A straight wrist also permits the maximum forearm movement before the rod passes beyond the vertical. The muscles which move the forearm are very much more powerful than those which move the wrist — by using them, Jack ensures that he puts the maximum energy available into the rod.

Let us digress here a moment, because wrist movement is the

bugbear of all good casting. Casting with a straight wrist is probably the most unnatural movement involved in fishing. More than half of all fishermen bend their wrist too much. A third lock their wrist so fiercely that all their forearm muscles are in tension and they tire themselves out with this muscular conflict. Only a few per cent keep their wrist relaxed and straight at the same time, as they should do.

Now let us look where the line is positioned after Jack's back cast. It has travelled above his head in a nice tight loop, imparted to it by that 'flick' of his and is stretched out behind him, slightly above the horizontal. Had he bent his wrist, the rod would have gone well past the vertical and the line would have been driven into the ground behind him. Jack has positioned it just right. When he starts the forward cast, the line will be travelling horizontally.

When, and only when, he feels a little tug on the rod, as the line reaches its furthest backward extension, Jack starts the forward cast by a slowly accelerating reversal of the backcast. When the rod reaches about 11 o'clock and there is a good bend in it, Jack crowds on the power again to about 10.30. After that, he lets his hand drift down until the rod-tip is, once more, pointing where the fly will fall. In the meantime, the line has taken on a tight forward loop, unrolled itself, plus the cast and the fly, so that all lie on a straight line about 3 ft above the water. From there they will drop gently down onto it.

Points to Watch
It cannot be stressed too strongly that *the overhead cast is made or broken on the quality of the back cast.* Failure in the back cast usually results from one or other of two simple faults.

It seems that the fisherman, having been provided with a wrist, feels he has got to bend it. He will not only swear to his instructor that he didn't bend it, but he will really be convinced that he didn't. I have personal experience of this because I used to do it myself! It was only when somebody showed me a film of my casting that I was convinced. Since then, I cannot tell you how many hours I have spent with the butt of the rod tucked into the cuff of my sleeve to stop me bending my wrist! If the fisherman does bend his wrist in the back cast, the rod goes well over the vertical and drives the line into the ground.

The second fault is, perhaps, easier to eradicate. It arises from the fact that the fisherman is so anxious to cast his line forward that he does not complete the back cast — he does not allow the line to extend fully behind him. He may not even give it enough impetus to do so. More often than not, the impetus is there, but the forward cast commences too soon. The line does not come forward properly because power is applied to a sloppy line, and a line must be tight before it will accept that power. In addition, enormous strains are set up in the line, sufficient for a fly weighing a grain or two to break a cast of 10 lb breaking strain. As the line finally catches up with the premature movement of the rod a sonic crack is heard because the line exceeds the speed of sound. This may not only break the leader but also causes cracks of a different kind to develop in the coating of the line.

Practice and Accuracy

The beginner should start, if he can, with his line out on water. Practice on grass does not involve the same drag as that of a line being picked off water. Ideally, the equipment used should be an 8' or 8' 3" rod which takes a #6 line. It is a mistake to start with either too light or too heavy equipment. An 8' 3" rod, carrying a #6 line, could be described as the perfect average tackle for all single-handed fly casting.

Start practicing the back cast until you have mastered it. Don't worry that the line falls onto the ground behind you at the end of each exercise. Develop the ability to throw about 20 ft of line up behind you, to its full length, a little above the horizontal. Practice until you have that action looking right and, perhaps more importantly, feeling right, with a tell-tale tug manifesting itself as the line reaches its full extension. Once you feel you have mastered the back cast, you may combine it with the forward cast. First of all, be content to be able to cast your line to its full 20 ft in front of you. When that is right, try to cast it so that the fly hovers 2 or 3 ft above the water before it drops onto it.

The time has now come to look for more accuracy of direction. There are three basic ways in which the exact spot can be missed. The fly is either too far to the right or left; it is either too far or too short of the target; or it has been driven into the water or high in the air. If you follow Jack's practice of bringing the thumb up to the eye, you can use that as a sight, like the rear sight of a gun and eliminate errors to right and left of target. Problems of distance involve aerialising exactly the right length of line, and this is achieved by false casting in the air until the fly is going out exactly over the target. Elimination of the final possibility of error, the driving of the line into the water or too high, comes with practice.

It is probably most convenient to practice casting for accuracy on dry ground. Choose a windy day, place a handkerchief or newspaper weighted down with a stone on a lawn or field which gives ample room to move around it. Starting at one point about 30 or 40 ft away from the target, cast to it two or three times until it has been hit. Move round it, two paces at a time, repeating the exercise. You will thus be able to appreciate and master the effect of the wind, coming from every quarter, as you work round. This, I think, is the only occasion when practicing on dry ground has any advantage over practicing on water.

Until now, the line has been held against the handle of the rod with the index finger and it is time to bring the other hand into play. Its function in single-handed casting is to control the line in relation to the rod.

The Line Hand

In the initial stage of the cast Jack had the rod pointing at the fly and 20 ft of line and leader out on the water. Let us suppose that the line lies in loose coils and is thoroughly slack. He can remedy that by reaching forward with his left hand, towards the butt ring of the rod, grasping the line with his finger and thumb and gently pulling it in. If he does this sufficiently, then from the moment he starts to lift the rod the load will come onto it and the result will be that the back cast is not only tidier but more effective too, because energy is being stored in the rod, by bending, at an earlier stage.

The work of the line hand increases in importance as he casts further. Its main function must be to maintain the line in tension. To that end, and particularly when he is making a retrieve, he lets the line run over the index finger of the right hand and uses that finger pressed against the cork as a brake. It also acts as a line locator, so that the left hand can find the line without Jack looking for it. It maintains tension on the line, while the left hand shifts its position to take another length of line. That ensures that Jack is ready to react immediately to a 'take' at all times.

Disposal of the slack line drawn in by the left hand is achieved by one of three established methods:

(a) Large loops hanging over the left hand are formed and held in position by the left thumb.
(b) Where very slow retrieves are involved, the line is taken into the palm in a series of figure-of-eight loops created by movement of the left fingers.
(c) The line is stripped into a line tray onto the water or onto the ground.

Whatever method is adopted, it must be such that it will permit

the feeding back of the line through the rod-rings for false casting
or 'shooting' line.

False Casting

False casting involves precisely the same movements as the
overhead cast, but instead of allowing the line to fall on the water
at the end of the forward cast it is drawn straight back from its
position two or three feet above the water into another back cast and
a further forward cast. During this process extra line may be
allowed to slide between the index finger of the right hand and the
rod butt, feeding itself through the rings of the rod and into the air.
This is done at either end of the false cast, the amount being
released at each cast depending on vigour and effectiveness of the
casting operation.

Having mastered the movements of the overhead cast, the time
has now come to develop it. Start with the line passing between the
index finger of the right hand and the rod butt, with the minimum
amount of line beyond the rod-tip. As the rod comes back into the
back cast, clamp the line to the cork handle with the right index
finger and pull off extra line from the reel with the left hand. On the
next forward cast, lift the index finger from the cork, allowing the
line to slide through the fingers of the left hand as it shoots up
through the rings and extends the aerialised portion. Repeat the
process on the next back and forward cast and gradually work more
and more line into the air from the reel. You will be surprised at the
amount of line you can aerialise, very quickly indeed, by this
method.

False casting should only be continued long enough to aerialise
sufficient line or to dry the fly. Two false casts are enough for the
latter. Excessive false casting leads to premature line breakdown. I
once counted a very good fly fisherman make no less than 28 false
casts. Later, in the course of conversation, I brought the subject
round to the number of false casts one might reasonably make and
he told me he normally made 3 or 4!

With, against and across Wind

If the wind is in your face, put in your power arc a little earlier in the
back cast and a little later in the forward cast. This prevents the
wind from dragging the line into the ground behind you on the
back cast. Equally, delaying the power arc in the forward cast helps
you to drive it in under the wind. If you follow this rule exactly, and
do not alter your casting technique in any other way, you will be
amazed how easy it is to cast into the wind.

When you cast *with* the wind delay the power arc in your back cast in order to drive the line back behind you, under the wind, and start your forward power arc early. The wind will lift your line and carry it out in front of you.

If a cross-wind is running from left to right, you have only to turn and cast a little into the wind to ensure that the fly arrives where you want it. If the wind is running from right to left, there is really only one safe thing to do and that is to cast left-handed.

Left-hand casting should be learnt and practiced by every fisherman. It makes cross-wind casting safe, for it ensures that the fly will always be carried away from you. There are, also, innumerable occasions on which riverside obstructions make it desirable to be able to use your left hand. Some fishing books describe many fancy combinations of casts as a substitute for left-hand casting. These are quite unnecessary as left-hand casting itself is a very simple operation which is easily learned.

Once you have mastered the right hand overhead cast, you can teach your left hand to do the same, by putting a rod in each hand and casting with both of them at once. The rods should, of course, be the same size and carry the same length of line. A few minutes of trial will prove to you, beyond doubt, that this is not difficult. Once you have mastered the art of casting with two rods together drop that from your right hand and take hold of the line with it. You will find you can manage the left-hand cast in exactly the same way as the right-hand one. It is a source of wonderment to me that so much is made of left-hand casting. If you use your right hand, to teach your left hand, the thing is so very, very simple. Next time you go to a Game Fair watch the professionals casting with rods in both hands. You will be able to hear the praise of the crowd, with the satisfied knowledge that you can do it too!

Accelerating the Line
Let us now study some of the variants of the overhead cast. More speed can be given to the line, in either the forward cast or the back cast, by pulling the line through the rod rings as the power arc is applied. The line is thus given an additional impulse, beyond that given by the rod. Try giving a little tug as you pick the line off the water and another as you put in the power on the forward cast. Once that seems to be going smoothly and rhythmically let the line go at the end of the power arc on the forward cast. It will shoot through the rings and increase the distance of your cast. It pays to practice these left-hand pulls until you are really confident that you have got the timing quite right. Once you are sure of this you can

move on to the double haul cast, which was designed to achieve the maximum distance possible.

The Horizontal Cast

The so-called horizontal cast is really an overhead cast, performed in a horizontal plane instead of in a vertical one. Between these two planes one can use the same casting technique at any angle that happens to be convenient, in any given circumstances of fishing.

Overcoming Drag

When casting a dry fly across fast water onto slow water, the fly can be very quickly dragged as a result of the 'belly' put in the line by faster water. This can be met by dropping the line on the water, loose. To do this, either check the line in the air when it is fully extended with a little tug of the left hand, or deliberately overcast, i.e. put more energy into your cast than the length of line you are actually casting makes necessary. Another method, which has its dangers, is to make a little up-stream mend of the line. That is, to give the rod a little up-stream flick just as the line hits the water. This can be dangerous because you can quite easily snatch the fly from the fish's mouth if it is not done properly. Yet another method, which takes a lot of practicing, is to wave the rod gently right and left as it drifts down after the power arc. Mending is also important when fishing a wet fly across and down, both for single- and double-handed casting. The fly will only fish well when it is hanging below the line. It must be facing into the current. In order that it may do so, as quickly as possible, it is desirable to mend the line. Mending is achieved by giving the line an up-stream flick as it touches the water. This causes the belly of the line to take an upstream arc so that the tip of the line and fly swim against the stream and not across it. When a sinking line is used mending makes the fly fish deeper.

THE DOUBLE HAUL CAST

For the double haul cast Jack stands with his left foot forward and with his weight on this foot. He is either using a weight-forward (forward-taper) line, or better still, a shooting head backed with nylon. All the belly of the forward taper line, and the whole of the shooting head, will be outside the tip-ring of the rod. A further two or three feet, either of running line or backing line, will also extend through the tip-ring.

Jack first makes sure there is no slack in the system. If there is he takes it up by pulling the line through the rings with his left hand. He then commences to lift the line from the water. His right arm, with the rod butt lying along his forearm and the wrist straight, as in the overhead cast, now comes up much higher. As soon as the rod begins to bend he starts piling on the power with both hands. His right hand accelerates the rod, while his left hand, by pulling downwards quite viciously on the line, both accelerates the line and puts further energy into the bending of the rod-tip. These movements bring the rear taper of the weight-forward line, or the butt of the shooting head, back to the rod-tip. Jack's right hand is now level with the top of his head and he continues to apply power well past the vertical, in fact, to about 12.30.

Added effort is being put into the whole movement, starting way down from his left toes, passing up through his left leg and into his body, thence, on up into his right arm. As his right hand goes beyond the vertical he transfers the weight from the left foot onto the right.

Once the rod has reached 12.30 he allows the line to drift out behind him. His left hand, still holding the line, follows this movement up towards the butt ring of the rod. This left hand movement re-aerialises the yard of line which he has pulled through the rod rings with that first vicious left hand pull.

What has all this achieved? First, he has added the whole power of his body from his left toe to his right hand, in moving the rod backwards and accelerating it. To that movement he has added a further substantial component by dragging the line through the rod rings. This has resulted in the line travelling to the rear, at a very much higher speed than in the overhead cast. At the end of its rearward journey it has replaced the small tug of the overhead cast with a rod bending pull, storing a great deal of energy in the rod.

At the point where this pull has caused the maximum bending of the rod, Jack begins his forward cast. He draws his right elbow towards his side, bringing the butt of the rod back along his forearm, from which it has been separated a little during the rearward drift. He now puts in a further rod bending pull, with his left hand.

Power now develops all the way from his right toes, through his body and into his right hand as he 'walks' his weight forward onto the left foot. As he does this, his right hand begins to stretch upwards and forwards, communicating the maximum acceleration to the rod and line. When the rod reaches the 10 o'clock position his left hand lets go of the line. This allows the rod to pull out as much loose running, or backing line, as possible into a 'shoot'. Finally,

54

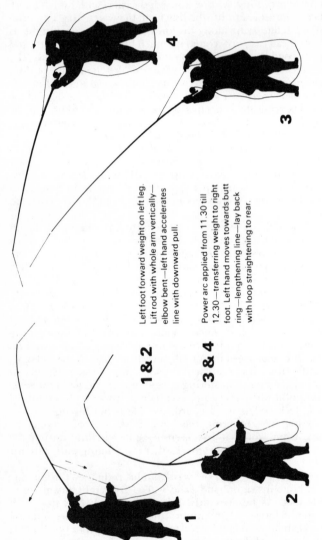

1 & 2 Left foot forward weight on left leg. Lift rod with whole arm vertically—elbow bent—left hand accelerates line with downward pull.

3 & 4 Power arc applied from 11.30 till 12.30—transferring weight to right foot. Left hand moves towards butt ring—lengthening line—lay back with loop straightening to rear.

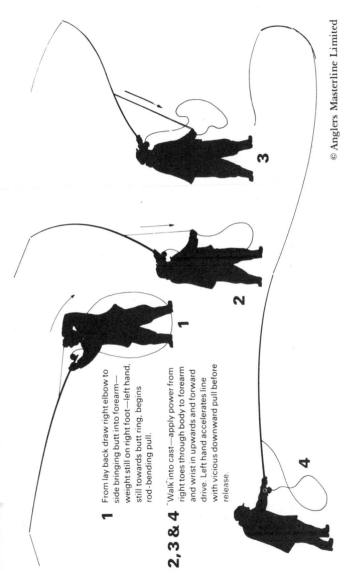

1 From lay back draw right elbow to side bringing butt into forearm—weight still on right foot—left hand still towards butt ring, begins rod-bending pull.

2, 3 & 4 "Walk" into cast—apply power from right toes through body to forearm and wrist in upwards and forward drive. Left hand accelerates line with vicious downward pull before release.

© Anglers Masterline Limited

8. & 9. (Top) *the double haul back cast*, and (bottom) *the forward cast*

he allows the right hand and rod to follow through and down until it is pointing, as in the overhead cast, to the fly on the water.

Unfortunately, the double haul cast, though extremely popular with reservoir bank fishermen, is rarely performed well. Properly done, it is compact, elegant, precise and can bring the fly down on the water as gently as the conventional overhead cast. Nothing is is gained by false casting and aerialising line outside the rod-tip. Further extension puts enormous strains on rod and line and does not help the achievement of an extra foot. If the backing line or running line is carefully arranged either in the water, on the bank or in a line tray, then shooting the line achieves far greater distance with the added advantage of complete control of its behaviour in the air.

Mastering the left-handed double haul cast is, I am afraid, more difficult than is the case with the simple overhead cast. Obviously, the right hand cannot be used to teach the left, for it is occupied in pulling the line. Even so, the effort and time involved in learning to double haul with both hands is well worth the practice for stillwater fishermen.

THE ROLL CAST

The most important feature of the roll cast is that the fly never travels behind the caster. It is therefore particularly useful when there are obstructions behind, and the back cast cannot therefore be used. Furthermore, the overhead cast and the roll cast, either separately or jointly, form the basis of all fly casting, and are therefore essential in the flyfisherman's repertoire.

Let us look at Jack. His stance is the same as for the overhead cast. He draws in the line, skidding it on the top of the water by raising his forearm and elbow. The elbow is not used as a fulcrum. Jack's hand travels to a position about head height, with the rod at about 1 o'clock. He is not applying any power and when the rod reaches the highest point he keeps it there until the line forms a loose loop down from the tip and slightly behind him. That loop is the absolute essential first stage of the roll cast. Jack now starts the forward cast quite slowly, accelerating as for the overhead cast. His power arc does not commence until very late indeed, certainly no earlier than 10 o'clock. It is very short and, compared with the overhead cast, very powerful. It is this late powerful thrust that starts that essential loop on its rolling path across the water. In due course it travels far enough to lift the fly from the water so that the final presentation is similar to, and as gentle as, that of the overhead

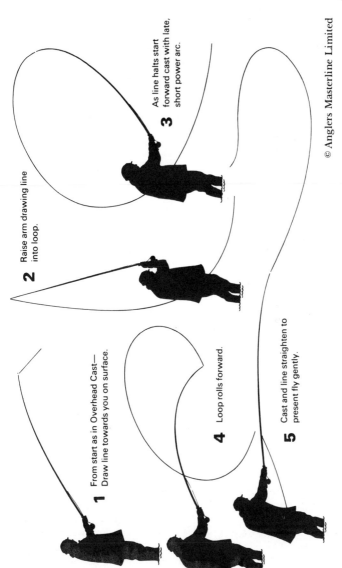

1 From start as in Overhead Cast—Draw line towards you on surface.

2 Raise arm drawing line into loop.

3 As line halts start forward cast with late, short power arc.

4 Loop rolls forward.

5 Cast and line straighten to present fly gently.

10. *The roll cast*

© Anglers Masterline Limited

cast. The roll cast has another very valuable function — it can be used to roll a sinking line up onto the surface, making it ready to be picked off cleanly into a normal overhead cast, prior to a new presentation. Once mastered, the line can even be rolled right up into the air so that there is no splash at the point of pick off, which might scare fish.

When some obstruction exists behind the caster, the line can be first extended by shaking a few yards out onto the water. A short roll cast is made, with further line going through the rings as the power arc is applied. This process can be repeated as often as is necessary, until the fish are covered.

TWO-HANDED CASTING

A great mystique is made of two-handed casting for salmon. In fact, if you have mastered both the single-handed overhead cast, and the roll cast, you have also mastered the basic movements of all two-handed fly casting.

In the overhead, double-handed cast, the left hand is used solely as a fulcrum. The palm should be open, upwards, and the butt of the rod rests in it and is lightly held there by the finger and thumb. Its position should be level with the heart and movement is permitted in the back cast, forwards from the heart but not by more than 9″. This movement is reversed and the hand brought back to the heart on the forward cast. The right hand is situated on the rod, the width of the shoulders from the butt. The position of the hand, is, as in the overhead cast, with the thumb pointing up the rod and the weight carried between the thumb and the fingers with the line clamped to the cork by the index finger. The line can also be held by the left hand too.

All the power of the cast is supplied by the right hand and arm. The movement is the same as in the overhead cast. A slow start, the piling on of power at about 10.30, the bringing of the hand up level with the eye and the drift to the rear are exactly repeated. Since the fulcrum is on the left side of the fisherman, the path of the rod will be in a plane at a slight angle to the vertical.

The forward cast sequence is, again, exactly as in the single-handed overhead cast. The power is put in at about 11 o'clock, completed by 10 o'clock, and the line allowed to roll out and drift down to the water with the rod-tip following it down and pointing to the fly.

This cast should be practiced until it can be done with either the left or the right hand as the fulcrum. The two-handed roll cast is so exactly like the single-handed roll cast as to need no further description.

THE SPEY CAST

The spey cast, which is a useful and very elegant form of roll cast, should, perhaps, be described in more detail. Its purpose is to roll out a long line from a position where there is no possibility of making a back cast.

Let us take the case when the river is flowing from right to left and the wind is from left to right. The fisherman stands facing the point where he wishes to place the fly. As his fly 'fishes out', i.e. as it swings across the river and below him, he follows it with his rod-tip and swivels his body from the hips in the same direction without moving his feet. When the fly is finally 'on the dangle' below him, he draws in sufficient line to leave a manageable length beyond the rod-tip. Then he lifts the rod vertically above his right shoulder with his right hand uppermost. This lifts as much of the line clear of the water as is possible. Then, swivelling his body back to the front again and facing the spot at which he wishes to cast, he pulls the line forward and round, by dipping the rod-tip in a shallow arc, before raising it high again over his right shoulder. This should bring the fly a few yards to his right front, on top of the water. His position now is that of a man about to make a forward roll cast and the line should develop that all-essential loop on his right-hand side.

The rest of the spey cast is a perfectly normal roll cast from that position, with its late power arc rolling the line across the water, until the fly finally reaches its destination. The power arc should be allowed to drag any line necessary through the rod rings to permit the fly to reach the desired position.

I have described the spey cast in three stages. That is, clearing the line, as far as possible, from the water; flicking the fly to the right side; and the roll cast finish. In fact, it should be one continuous rhythmic movement from start to finish and, when you have it right, it feels very good indeed!

When the river runs from left to right and the wind from right to left, it is necessary to have the left hand up the rod and to make the final delivery from above the left shoulder.

Complications occur when wind and river flow in the same direction. Personally, I prefer to ensure, if possible, that I cast from the shoulder that is downwind, even though it may be down river too. Generally speaking, it is however a question of judging the degree to which wind and water affect the fly. If the wind is strong and the stream weak, let wind prevail and vice versa.

It is impossible to practice a spey cast away from the river. Without the drag of a stream, both timing and execution suffer to such a degree as to make the practice worthless. Do be careful that you have got the fly on that side of the body where your hand is uppermost. Salmon flies are quite heavy things and though I have never experienced it I think that to hook your own nose might be very, very painful!

This chapter has concentrated on technique. It is not intended to replace practice and formal instruction from a professional instructor. All who wish to take up fly fishing will find that investment in at least a short course from a professional will yield them invaluable dividends in the form of future enjoyment. My hope is that this chapter will help them to understand good casting technique and to profit the more from such personal instruction.

Taff Price

The Natural Flies &
their Imitation

The larder of the trout embraces most of the insect groups. It can be a highly selective feeder, much to the frustration of the angler, but it is not fastidious and takes equal delight in feeding on delicate Mayflies, the blackest of beetles or the spindliest of Craneflies. This chapter therefore covers most groups of insect, though for completeness it also includes other creatures such as snails and tadpoles which are eaten by trout.

Over the years the ingenuity and skill of flydressers have yielded thousands of fly patterns to imitate the many different creatures which make up the trout's diet. Obviously, in order to select the right fly, it is an advantage to know what our quarry is feeding on, and this can be often done simply by observation. Too many anglers fish without giving a thought to the insects which are hatching out all around them, and much of this chapter aims to give the fisherman enough information to enable him to match his fly to the natural insect.

When a fish is caught, confirmation of its diet can be obtained by sampling the contents of its stomach with a long thin spoon called a marrow spoon. The resulting sludge is then placed in a shallow white dish and analysed. A modern equivalent of the marrow spoon extracts the stomach contents by means of a teat dropper and discharges them into a test-tube. Also, a full autopsy during cleaning a fish often shows a wealth of creatures that can be copied at the fly-tying bench and used to good effect.

Before embarking on a detailed description of the various insects and other creatures that have been imitated by fly-dressers, the subject of imitating the trout's diet should be considered. It is one of the most controversial areas of fly fishing which never ceases to attract argument and discussion. Traditional schools of thought argued for exact imitation, whereas more modern ideas are less strict. Whatever the truth — and it is almost impossible to settle most disputes — it is true that a knowledge of entomology adds very considerably to a fisherman's ability to catch fish. More importantly, it adds a new dimension to his sport and provides endless opportunity for observation and experiment.

THE UP-WINGED FLIES

These are the flies beloved by the chalk-stream angler, and the development of fly fishing and fly dressing owes a lot to their study. To talk of the hatch or the evening rise is to talk about these delicate insects, the Mayflies or Ephemeroptera.

There are about 41 known species of Ephemeroptera in Britain, of which the more common are the Large and Small Dark Olives,

Ephemeroptera

Plecoptera

Trichoptera

Diptera

11. *Silhouettes of some natural flies shown alongside imitations of them*

DRY FLIES 6 Winged. 6 Hackled.

Winged

reenwell's Glory.

Ginger Quill.

Winged Pheasant Tail.

Sedge.

Daddy Longlegs (or Crane Fly).

Lunn's Sherry Spinner.

Hackled

Coch-y-Bonddu.

Blue Upright.

Soldier Palmer.

Kite's Imperial.

Red Tag.

Tup's Indispensable.

WET FLIES 3 Winged. 3 Hackled. 6 "Attractors".

Winged

March Brown.

Olive Dun.

Alder.

Hackled

Snipe & Purple.

Partridge & Yellow.

Half Stone.

Attractors

Jungle Alexandra.

Golden Olive.

Butcher.

Woodcock & Green.

Peter Ross.

Invicta.

Blue Winged Olive, Iron Blue, Mayfly (Grey or Green Drake), Caenis, Lake Olive, Pond Olive and Pale Watery. Depending on the species, this group of insects is found in both running and still waters from the smallest pond to the largest reservoir, from insignificant ditches to the most regal of rivers.

General Identification and Life Cycle

Four wings, the hind pair very small or practically non-existent, held upright over the body. Bodies long and slender, antennae very small, 2 or 3 long tails. Length from 6 to 25 mm, though most species are about 12 mm long. Life cycle:

egg ⟶ nymph ⟶ dun ⟶ spinner

The nymph. Eggs are laid by the female in a number of different ways, depending on the species. Some descend aquatic vegetation to lay the eggs below the surface, whereas others lay them by dipping the tips of their abdomen below the surface. The eggs hatch out into the larval stage, or nymph, which generally spends about 12 months in water (larger species spend a lot longer). Some nymphs are good swimmers, while others are flattened and possess almost crab-like legs for clinging to rocks in fast water. Yet others are adapted for digging or burrowing into the silt, and the nymph of the Mayfly itself possesses the very powerful legs of a typical digger. Some nymphs spend their entire lives in aquatic vegetation, feeding on algae and never venturing very far from their safe green haven.

When it is time for the nymph to hatch, air builds up under its outer shell, causing it to rise to the surface, where it quickly splits its infant skin and emerges on the surface as the dun.

The dun. The dun, or sub-imago to give it its entomological name, is peculiar to this group of insects alone. It takes the place of the pupal stage which occurs in many other insect groups, and is probably an evolutionary relic, for the Ephemerids are one of the most primitive insect groups. The newly emerged dun floats serenely on the surface drying its wings and it is very vulnerable at this time. The trout feed greedily on these infant flies and it is only those which reach the safety of the bankside trees and shrubs that proceed to the final metamorphosis. Their outer skin splits and a beautiful adult fly emerges known to the fisherman as the spinner.

The spinner. This is the final stage in the short life of the adult Mayfly. At dusk, clouds of male spinners are often seen dancing in the twilight, and as the females arrive mating takes place on a first-

12. *The life cycle of the Mayfly*

come-first-served basis! The unfortunate male soon dies and more often than not falls onto the ground, though some in fact fall onto the water. The female goes on to lay her eggs before she too falls dead on the water — and so the cycle goes on. For the angler the spent spinner is perhaps one of the most killing flies. Suggested artificial flies for imitating the various stages of the Ephemeroptera are shown opposite.

The March Brown. The Ephemeroptera cannot be left without mentioning this member of the family that is used by fishermen the world over. The March Brown has been copied and used effectively by anglers from the north of Scotland to the tip of Cornwall.

However, the natural March Brown occurs on very few rivers and so it must be assumed that the trout mistake the fly for some other insect, or are attracted by the 'all round edible appearance' of the dressing.

SUGGESTED ARTIFICIALS FOR THE UP-WINGED FLIES

Type of fly	Nymph	Dun	Spinner
The Olives (Large, Small & Medium) and the Lake Olive	Olive Nymph, Sawyer's Pheasant Tail Nymph	Blue Dun, Blue Upright, Rough Olive, Greenwell's Glory, Gold-Ribbed Hare's Ear & various named Olive patterns	Pheasant Tail, Lunn's Particular
The Blue Winged Olive	As above	Various named B.W.O. patterns	Sherry Spinner
The Mayfly	Various named Mayfly patterns	Grey & Green Drake, French Partridge Mayfly, Straddlebug	Various Spent Mayfly patterns
The Iron Blue	Iron Blue Nymph or any dark coloured nymph	Various named Iron Blue patterns	Pheasant Tail, Houghton Ruby, Jenny Spinner (imitates the male)
Pale Watery	Tup's Nymph	Tups, Goddard's Last Hope	Lunn's Yellow Boy, Lunn's Particular, Ginger Quill
Caenis	Small patterns of Sawyer's Nymphs	No patterns as life of dun is so brief	Various named Spinner patterns
Pond Olive	Olive Nymph	As for other Olives	Apricot Spinner

THE ROOF-WINGED FLIES

The Sedge or Caddis flies belong to the family Trichoptera, meaning hairy-winged. There are about 190 different species in Britain, many of which are of no interest to the angler because they are either too small or very localised in their habitat. The Sedge flies have been copied by flydressers since the dawn of fly fishing, and are good flies to use at dusk, for it is then that most species hatch out. For the record, there is one species which is totally terrestrial, spending both larval and adult forms out of water.

General Identification and Life Cycle
Moth-like in appearance, wings held like a roof over the back; long antennae, sombre coloration (mostly shades of brown). No tails and four wings. Often found resting on bankside vegetation, usually flies at dusk.

egg ⟶ larva (caddis) ⟶ pupa ⟶ adult

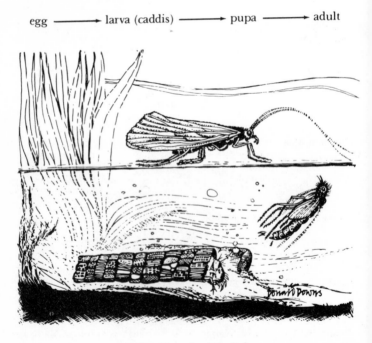

13. *The life cycle of the Sedge*

The caddis larva. The female Sedge lays her eggs in a number of different ways, depending on the species. Some fly over the water and release a sticky ball of eggs, whereas others lay them on overhanging bushes, leaving the infant larvae to emerge and drop into the river. Yet other species dip the tips of their abdomen below the surface, whilst others crawl down reed-stems and lay their eggs directly on the gravel of the river bed.

The infant larvae soon hatch out and begin to adapt to their environment in various ways. Most build for themselves those protective cases which are so well known, using a variety of materials — fine grains of sand stuck together with a sticky secretion from the larva; pebbles; vegetable matter such as duckweed or reed; and sometimes awkward-shaped twigs to make it difficult for predators to eat them. In some instances the heavier pebbles form a built-in ballast to prevent the creature from being washed away by the current, and to keep them close to the river bed.

Not all members of the Sedge family build cases — some build nothing at all until it is time to pupate, when a rough covering of stones stuck to a larger rock seems to suffice. Others create webs or funnels for the same reason as spiders — to protect them and also to trap food.

When they pupate the caddis larvae seal themselves in their shelters. The pupa subsequently breaks out of the shelter, floats to the surface, splits its skin and the adult insect emerges.

The adult Sedge. The lifespan of the adult is about 7 days. The trout usually takes the Sedge at the point of hatching, for it is some while before its wings are dry enough to allow flight, and it is then at its most vulnerable. The newly hatched insect runs across the water surface — anglers say 'skitters' — producing quite a disturbance and a miniature wake which alerts the trout and presumably triggers off its feeding response. It is usual for anglers to fish the artificial Sedge in the same way, hoping for the same response from the trout.

Unlike the Mayflies, many of the artificial and natural Sedges have the same name. A few of the more common Sedges that are copied in fur and feathers and used by anglers are given below.

SUGGESTED ARTIFICIALS FOR THE ROOF-WINGED FLIES

The Silver Sedge, Brown Sedge, Grannom or Greentail, Red Sedge, Great Red Sedge, Grey Flag, Cinnamon Sedge, Welshman's Button, Caperer, Black Silverhorn, Brown Silverhorn, Grouse Wing Sedge, Ronald's Sand Fly

THE HARD-WINGED FLIES

The Stoneflies or Plecoptera are so called from their habit of resting on stones in and around the river. They inhabit the swift-flowing crystal rivers of moor and mountain, and are also found on the chalk streams, on which it would be true to say that they are virtually ignored in favour of the illustrious Mayflies. However, they become an important source of food for trout on those streams where the Ephemeroptera are somewhat scarce. It is not usual to find Stoneflies in any numbers on slow-moving rivers — they need an environment rich in oxygen and are extremely susceptible to all forms of pollution. Water abstraction, by reducing the flow of the stream or river, has a similar effect.

There are about 34 different species of Stonefly in Britain, ranging from 7 to 12 mm in length. The largest British species has a larva of 25 mm and an adult of 18 mm, though in the fast-flowing rivers of the Western States of the U.S.A. they attain a length of 60 mm.

General Identification and Life Cycle

Four wings, slender bodies, two tails (this also applies to the larva, unlike the British Ephemerid nymphs which always have three tails). Some species have heavily veined wings that lie flat across their backs, others tend to roll their wings as one author put it 'like rolled-up umbrellas'. They are extremely poor fliers and the males of some species have such rudimentary wings that they cannot fly at all. Sombre-coloured, usually brown, with the exception of two species, the Yellow Sally and the Little Yellow Sally, which are a distinctive bright yellow. They are usually seen on stones and boulders in and around the river, or hiding away on shady moss or in the crevices of bark. They mate on the ground.

egg ⟶ larva (creeper) ⟶ adult

The creeper. The larvae are called creepers and remain in the water from one to three years depending on the species. The larger species spend longer at the creeper stage. Like the adult insect, the creeper is not a very adventurous soul, preferring to hide itself away in the gravel or under stones. In the Northern counties fishing the live creeper has long been a successful method of catching trout.

When it is time for the creeper to change into the adult form it crawls out of the river onto boulders or up onto the bank where it splits out of its skin, dries its wings and then either weakly flies off or runs helter-skelter to the nearest shady haven.

14. *The life cycle of the Stonefly*

The adult stonefly. This insect seldom ventures far from water and is usually found hiding down in the grass-roots or in the shady reed-stems away from strong light. The life of the adult fly is approximately four weeks and it exists solely to procreate. The female stonefly returns to the water to release her sticky ball of eggs by inserting the tip of her abdomen below the surface.

Anglers have invented their own names for some of the more common Stoneflies (*see* below) and fortunately most of the artificials go by the same names. Most of the flies are fished wet as sparsely dressed 'spider' patterns.

SUGGESTED ARTIFICIALS FOR STONEFLIES

The Yellow Sally, Little Yellow Sally, Willow Fly, Needle Brown (or Spanish Needle), February Red (or Old Joan), Large Stonefly

THE FLAT-WINGED FLIES

The Flat-winged or 'true' flies belong to the large and very variable class of insects known entomologically as the Diptera. There are more than 5 000 different species of this class in Britain, the bulk of which are of no interest to the angler whatsoever. However, a high proportion do spend their larval stage in water and therefore figure in the diet of the trout.

Craneflies, Gnats, Midges, Mosquitoes, Hawthorn flies, Cow-dung flies, Houseflies, Bluebottles etc. — all are true flies that have been copied by flydressers and used with success on rivers and still waters. At certain times of year these insects can be an important source of food for trout and imitations of them often prove killing when all other flies seem to fail.

Though flies such as the Hawthorn fly can be an effective and important pattern for the river angler, it is on still waters that the Diptera come into their own. The Chironomid Midge or Buzzer is perhaps the most important source of food for fish on all still waters, on which they greatly outnumber any other insect.

A general description of an insect group as diverse in shape. size, and habits cannot be given. However, they all have something in common — two wings and no tails. Some characteristic and well-known groups will now be considered.

The Chironomid Midge

There are about 400 different species of Chironomid Midge in Britain, varying in size from 1 to 15 mm. Their colours include olive, grey-black, bright green, orange, red — in fact most natural colours. The life cycle is:

egg $\longrightarrow$ larva (bloodworm) $\longrightarrow$ pupa $\longrightarrow$ adult

The bloodworm. The blood red colour of this larva is due to the haemoglobin it needs to carry oxygen around its body, for its habitat is deep in the lake, down in the mud where the oxygen levels are very low. Other midge larvae are coloured yellow, cream and various shades of green. The bloodworm lives in tunnels in the mud, and they are fairly static, unlike the larvae of mosquitoes or the Phantom Midge which are free-swimming.

Natural bloodworm have always been considered very good hook bait for coarse fish such as roach or bream, and in fact their use has been banned in certain competitions.

The pupa. The pupal form of this insect is perhaps the stage best known to the fisherman. It wriggles and twitches its way to the surface where it hangs hooklike and wriggling in the surface film. At this stage large numbers are taken by trout. It has difficulty in penetrating the surface film, but once it has broken through it splits open and the adult midge emerges. In some species the insect's wings are a bright orange but the colour fades within seconds of contact with the air.

The adult midge. These delicate flies are seen hovering and dancing in large numbers over the water. In strong winds they are often blown a good distance away from the water. These swarms, looking like a gyrating grey mist, are usually the males of the species — the females bide their time close by on the bankside vegetation. Mating usually takes place a few hours after hatching, though on one occastion I witnessed coupling on the water as the females crawled out of the pupal shuck. The female lays her eggs by dropping them directly onto the water, and so the life cycle begins again.

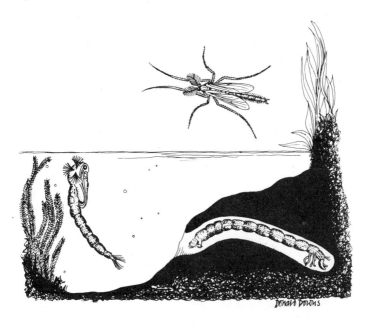

15. *The life cycle of the Chironomid Midge*

The Chironomid Midges are sometimes known as dancing gnats, though contrary to popular belief they neither sting nor bite.

SUGGESTED ARTIFICIALS FOR THE CHIRONOMID MIDGE

LARVA: Red or Green Larva, Marabou Bloodworm.
PUPA: Buzzer nymphs, Footballer, Blagdon Green Midge Pupa, Hatching Midge Pupa.
ADULT: Duckfly, Black Buzzer Midge, Blagdon Green Midge Adult, and named Chironomid patterns.

The Craneflies
The Daddy-long-legs is universally known but it is not so well known that there are about 300 British species of Cranefly. Many spend their larval stages in water while others are wholly terrestrial. Various species can be seen right through the fishing season, but it is in the month of September that they become popular with anglers. On some Irish limestone lakes the 'Daddy' is used to great effect as a live dapping fly during the latter half of the season. Another close relation of the Cranefly that enjoys a degree of popularity as a fishing fly is the Gravel Bed.

The Black Gnat
Most of these little dark-coloured terrestrial flies, collectively known as Black Gnats, belong to the genus *Bibio*. There are about 18 different British species. The Black Gnat used by anglers in springtime is thought to be *Bibio johannis* or *B. femrilis*, also known, quite unfairly as it happens, as the Fever Fly. Later in the year around September or October two or three other species make their appearance. But it doesn't matter a jot which gnat is which for when the trout appear to be taking small black flies put on a tiny Black Gnat — the trout do not differentiate so why should we?

The Hawthorn Fly
This fly is also a member of the genus *Bibio* and is a larger version of the Black Gnat. It is popular with the river angler, though even on some still waters it is blown onto the water in large numbers. The Hawthorn fly is easily recognised by its sluggish bumbling flight and its characteristic long trailing back legs. It is seen swarming around Hawthorn bushes, hence its common name.

A similar fly is the Bloody Doctor, *B. pomonae*, which has distinctive reddish coloured legs. This species makes its appearance

in June and is a popular fly in Scotland, Wales and The West
Country.

Various 'True' Flies

Many other true flies are copied by flydressers and on their day can
be very killing indeed. When the trout cannot be tempted with more
palatable looking flies one of those below may well do the trick. An
aquatic fly used on still waters but difficult to imitate is the
Phantom Midge, a little insect that is transparent in all its stages.

SUGGESTED ARTIFICIALS FOR OTHER DIPTERA

Housefly, Blowfly, Horsefly, Bluebottle, Greenbottle, Cow-dung Fly,
Drone Fly, Reed Smuts, Oakfly

BEETLES

Many beetles are aquatic in both larval and adult forms, but it has
always been the terrestrial beetles that the angler and flydresser has
copied — the beetles that drop into the water by accident or lumber
off the banks into the river. Ground beetles, Leaf beetles, Weevils,
Rove beetles — all have turned up in the stomachs of fish. But the
most important beetles for the angler are the ones that tend to
swarm at certain times of the year. One such species is the June Bug,
known also as the Field or Garden Chafer. Anglers however have
named this fly after the Welsh name — the Coch-y-Bonddu, derived
from *coch*, meaning red, and a corruption of *bol ddu*, meaning
black belly. Another beetle that is found in large numbers on
bankside vegetation, particularly in the white flowering Cow
Parsley, is the Soldier beetle, the commonest species being the Black
Tipped Soldier. All the Soldier beetles are usually seen from June
onwards. They are weak fliers and many of them are blown onto the
water. Some beetle artificials are given below.

SUGGESTED ARTIFICIALS FOR BEETLES

Coch-y-Bonddu, Marlow Buzz, Bracken Clock, Little Chap, Soldier Beetle,
Sailor Beetle, Fern Web, Black Beetle, Brown Beetle

MOTHS

The insect class Lepidoptera includes all the moths and butterflies. Like the beetles there are a number of moths that are aquatic in their larval forms, resembling in many ways the larvae of the Sedge flies. In most cases these aquatic moths are of little importance to the angler — it is the dusk-flying terrestrial moth that accidentally falls into the lake or river that receives the angler's attention. Moth 'flies' are particularly effective for all species of trout, including the daylight-shy sea-trout, and it is usual to fish them at dusk or through the night.

One of the traditional methods of night fly fishing practised in the North is fishing with the 'Bustard'. The Bustard — or more precisely the various Bustards — are a series of flies which are intended to represent a number of different moths. They should not be confused with those flies which are tied with feathers from a Bustard's wing which are used as wet lake or sea-trout patterns.

Moth artificials can be used effectively in the daylight hours under trees or in shady parts of the river. I never go to Wales or the West Country without a stock of the Coachman, which represents a moth of sorts. Other moth artificials include White Moth, Ermine Moth, Ghost Swift Moth and the series of Bustards.

THE ALDER

An artificial tied to present the adult Alder fly was considered by the author Charles Kingsley to be second to none — it was his favourite dry fly. There are two British species, one very common and the other comparatively rare. The more common, *Sialis lutaria*, is on the wing from the end of April through to June. It spends its larval life as a rapacious underwater predator. As an adult it is a harmless bumbling creature which seems not to know where to go, often flying straight at the angler and resting on his clothing. During the months of March and April the larva crawls out of the water to pupate in little holes in the ground. Within a week or so it hatches out into a large brown Sedge-like fly with heavily veined wings. The adult Alder is a fly mainly used by the river angler, while the larva is an effective early season stillwater pattern. Suggested artificials include named Alder patterns, Herefordshire Alder and the Bug Eyed Alder (Wales).

DRAGON AND DAMSEL FLIES

The adult insects of the class Odonata are not considered important by the angler, except that they enhance the places where we fish with their beautiful colours and spectacular and graceful flight. It is the larval form or nymph that is of interest, for during the summer months prior to hatching these become highly active and are preyed on avidly by trout. Most of the Odonata seem to favour the smaller waters and are therefore a particularly effective lure for the small 'put and take' fisheries which are becoming so popular.

The smaller, slimmer Damsel fly is the most common and it is with its larva that we generally fish — that's not to say that the larger fatter Dragonfly nymphs are not copied — indeed on some waters they are very killing. Most artificials are named simply Damsel or Dragonfly nymph or larva, but there are two broad-spectrum nymph patterns that are used to imitate many of the larger aquatic larvae which prove very effective in this context, namely, the Baddow Special and the Ombudsman, a fly devised by Brian Clarke to imitate everything from an Alder larva to a Dragonfly larva. All these large artificial nymphs are best fished slowly along the bottom.

THE FRESHWATER SHRIMP

Gammarus pulex, the angler's Freshwater Shrimp is not really a shrimp at all — it belongs to a class of creatures called the Amphipoda, which includes the common Sandhopper. It varies in size from 7 to 12 mm and has a wide range of colours — dark olive green, light olive, golden olive almost yellow, and during mating it has a distinct orange tinge. It lives in weedy areas and that is where the artificials are fished.

A near-relative of the Freshwater Shrimp is the Water Louse, Hog Louse or Water Slater to give it its three common names. This little animal greatly resembles its terrestrial counterpart, the Woodlouse. Both creatures are taken by trout, and there are a number of artificial flies which have been devised to imitate them, two of the most popular being John Goddard's Shrimper and C. F. Walker's Freshwater Louse. It is usual to fish the shrimp patterns as weighted flies.

THE WATER BOATMEN

These insects greatly resemble beetles but they are in fact members of the Hemiptera or true bugs. The most important member of this group for the angler (strangely enough one of the few insects that he correctly names) is the Lesser Water Boatman, the Corixa. This

insect, unlike most other aquatic bugs, is wholly herbivorous and
spends its time on the bottom of the pond or lake, coming up now
and again for air. It looks like a small bead of quicksilver, for it
retains its air supply on its abdomen by means of very fine hairs.
Most species inhabit the margins of the lake and can be fished from
the very start of the season. Some books recommend that they
should be used from June onwards, but the numbers of Corixae that
are found in the stomachs of caught fish in April suggest otherwise.
Suggested artificials include named Corixa patterns such as Silver
Corixa and Green Corixa, and Chompers.

A closely related group of insects is the Back-Swimmers, which
are carnivorous and even attack fish and tadpoles. A word of
warning: keep your fingers away from the mouthparts of these
insects — their bit is as painful as a wasp-sting! Larger patterns of
the Corixae suffice to imitate these insects.

ANTS

Though there are many ant species the angler is only concerned
with three — Black Ant, Red Ant and Brown Ant. The insect comes
into its own on those hot sultry days when they are on the wing. A
barometric signal must go out to the nests over a wide area, for have
you noticed that on such days in late summer wherever you go ants
seems to be on their nuptial flight? These flying ants are often
blown onto the water, so always have an ant or two tucked away in
your flybox, for one day you could be fishing when there is a fall of
ants. There is also a case for fishing an ant pattern when they are
not on the wing — a foraging Wood Ant must often forage too far
and end up as a trout's meal.

SPIDERS AND 'SPIDERS'

There are a number of spiders whose normal habitat is on or close
to the water, including the various species of Raft Spider, that skim
across the water like Pondskaters, and the Wolf spider which hunts
its prey amidst the grass-stalk jungle of the river bank. Both of these
creatures are sometimes taken by trout, but they are rarely imitated
by the angler. Of more interest is a group of 'spiders' which are
fished to great effect on the rivers of Scotland and the North of
England — flies such as the Partridge & Orange, Snipe & Purple,
Poult Bloa etc. — the list is almost endless. The description 'spider'
refers to the sparse style of dressing and in fact they represent a
number of insects such as Mayflies and Stoneflies.

Before leaving the spider mention must be made of its tiny cousins, the aquatic mites. These minute blobs of colour are often found swimming around the weed banks in a lake or pond. Many are red, some yellow, others green — all are eaten, by accident or design, by the trout, as the evidence of autopsies show. There are at least two modern fishing flies which are designed to imitate the largest of the mites, the Large Red Mite.

SNAILS

The various freshwater snails are an important addition to the trout's diet. The every-hungry fish find in the snail an easy meal which is always available. Most snails are found in weed, and the trout make continuous sorties to feed on them and any other shy creatures that hide in the apparent safety of the lush greenery. Pulmonate or air-breathing snails have to make their way to the surface from time to time, and there are a number of very effective fly patterns tied with the floating snail in mind, including Floating Snail (Cliff Henry) and the Deerhair Floating Snail. For an imitation of the subsurface snail, a slowly fished Black & Peacock Spider is as good as any.

GRASSHOPPERS

Grasshoppers are from the class Orthoptera, which also includes the Crickets. They have always been considered a fine livebait for dapping for trout or chub in small overgrown rivers, and every fly fishing country has its own grasshopper patterns. In the U.S.A. even the Cricket has not escaped the notice of the creative flydresser, though in Britain the equivalent species are shy secretive creatures which rarely find themselves in water. (There is a true bug called the Water Cricket which is sometimes fished, but it does not belong to the Orthoptera.)

In the 17th century Charles Cotton devised two different dressings to represent the Grasshopper, namely, the Green and the Dun Grasshopper.

TADPOLES

Every water has its share of tadpoles which are preyed on by a wide variety of creatures from beetles to our quarry the trout. Simply contrived dressings of the Tadpole (and it matters not whether they are frogs or toads) can prove very effective in late May through to June.

FISH

Most so-called lures, whether they are Streamer flies made with feathers or Bucktails made with hair, are in the main created to imitate small fish. Minnows, Sticklebacks, infant Roach, Perch and even the sharp-spined Miller's Thumb or Bullhead are all eaten by trout, and all of them have been imitated successfully by flydressers. It is not only the so-called cannibal trout that eat other fish — all trout can be pisciverous when the occasion arises. They have no qualms in eating the infant fish of their own species.

Most artificials are named after the fish they are meant to imitate, e.g. Roach fry, Perch fry etc. Add to these such lures as the Jersey Herd, various Polystickles and of course the renowned Muddler Minnow and we have a fair selection of lures with which to imitate the small fish. Even some of the strangely coloured patterns that have no counterpart in the British fish fauna are sometimes effective, for it is probable that trout are attracted to the lure by shape rather than colour.

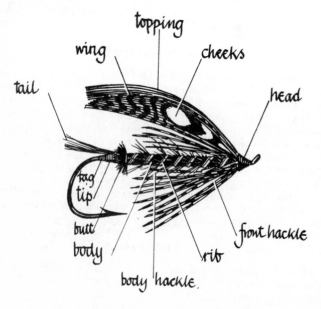

16. *Some flydressing terms illustrated*

John Veniard

The Craft of Fly-Tying

The insects which, at various stages of their life cycle, form part of the trout's diet are well described in the previous chapter. But to deceive the fish into thinking that what we offer them is the real thing, we must have sufficient skill and knowledge to reproduce something they will accept. Figure 16 shows the confection of fur and feather which the flydresser has devised to achieve this, and some of the terms which he uses to describe the various parts of an artificial fly. A glossary of many other terms used in flydressing will be found at the end of the chapter.

Although fly-tying is often referred to as an 'art', this is something of a misnomer — otherwise it would never have been possible to produce flies on a commerical basis. I prefer to describe it as a 'craft', and one which anyone can learn (with varying degrees of skill).

The earliest references we have to fly-tying take us back to 400 BC, but we had to wait until the 15th century for written accounts of these 'arts' in Britain. Dame Juliana Berners wrote *A Treatyse of Fysshynge wyth an Angle* in 1496, and gave dressings for a dozen flies, but it is only during the last hundred years or so that there has been such a keen interest in fly-tying on the scale we know today. Once considered a mere adjunct to fly fishing, fly-tying has now become a hobby in its own right.

During the leisurely period of the last half of the nineteenth century and the early years of the present one, many famous fishermen and fishing tackle firms contributed their knowledge and experience to making fly fishing the grand sport we know it to be. Today, this tradition is carried on by contemporary exponents of the skills of fly-tying such as Richard Walker, David Collyer, John Godard, Taff Price and many others who are only too willing to pass on the results of their painstaking experience.

MATERIALS AND EQUIPMENT

For making flies we have to call upon a considerable variety of materials, the most important of which are feathers from a wide range of birds, including game birds such as pheasant and partridge, wildfowl such as teal, mallard and widgeon, and — probably the most important of all — feathers from common poultry. Let me stress that none of these birds are killed specially for fly-tying — in fact the flydressing world depends almost entirely on the food trade for its materials, or uses feathers from such birds as crow, rook, jackdaw, jay and other enemies of the farmer.

When 'exotic' feathers are required, particularly for salmon flies, we are able to call on stocks of plumage from overseas, including peacock, kingfisher, bustard, golden pheasant, Amherst pheasant, heron, ostrich and macaw. In most instances the feathers we use are

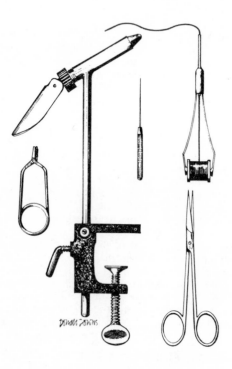

17. *Some fly-tying tools, including hackle pliars, a vice, dubbing needle and bobbin holder*

the result of moulting (peacock, ostrich and macaw) or once again, as in the case of the golden pheasant, are by-products from the food table.

In addition to feathers, we need fur for making bodies from the seal, hare, rabbit, mole, water rat and sheep. And from the tails of squirrel, deer, stoat and goat we obtain hair for certain types of wing. Finally, we must have certain essentials such as the hook of course, silks for tying, waxes and varnishes and more modern materials for bodies such as nylon, wools and tinsels (metallic and plastic) and innumerable odd items that the fertile imaginations of fly-tyers have conjured up.

Flies used to be tied with no mechanical aid other than a pair of scissors, but today we have such helpful items (*see* figure 17) as vices to hold the hook, hackle pliers for winding the feathers round the hooks, dubbing needles for picking out fur bodies, winging pliers for helping with the tricky task of putting on wings, bobbin holders to hold the reels of silk whilst they are in use, a whip finishing tool for tying off the head of flies, and even a guard to hold the hackle out of the way whilst the head of the fly is being varnished.

HOOKS AND THEIR TERMINOLOGY

The kind of fish to be caught, where it lives, and the type of fly to be used, must, of course, determine the type of hooks to use. A heavy hook in clear, placid water is as much out of place as a fine wire hook would be in heavy water where large fish can be expected. Furthermore, different sizes and patterns of hook must be used for

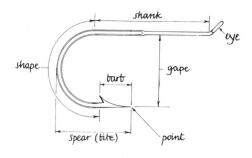

18. *Some terms used to describe a hook*

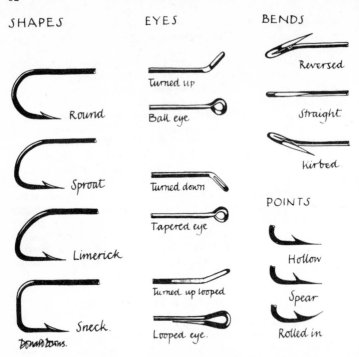

SHAPES

Round

Sproat

Limerick

Sneck.

DONALD DOWNS.

EYES

Turned up

Ball eye

Turned down

Tapered eye

Turned up looped

Looped eye.

BENDS

Reversed

Straight

Kirbed

POINTS

Hollow

Spear

Rolled in

19. *The major features of various kinds of hook*

different flies — streamer patterns, nymphs, etc., as no hook is appropriate for all styles of flyfishing. Figures 18 and 19 illustrate the various terms used to describe hooks, together with some of the various shapes widely used.

For dry-fly fishing, one of the best patterns of hook to use has a sproat shape, a turned-up eye, a slight reverse bend, and, of course, is made of light wire. An alternative, and second in popularity, is the same type of hook with a turned-down eye, although I think that much of its popularity is due to the fact that it is considered easier by some tyers to dress a fly on a hook with a downturned eye. Hooks with the round shape are also popular, in smaller sizes, for dry flies, but as the wire increases in weight in the larger sizes they become admirable for wet flies.

A good hook for all-round types of wet fly is the Limerick

pattern, which is usually made of quite stout wire.

Salmon flies can be divided up into four main groups, depending on the hook used: those using standard hooks which have a Dublin or Limerick Bend; summer or low-water hooks which are of lighter wire and longer in the shank for the same gape; dry-fly hooks which are of very light wire and which can also be used for low-water flies, and trebles for use with the now very popular tube flies. The standard and low-water hooks are also used as 'doubles'.

TYPES OF ARTIFICIAL FLY

There are literally hundreds — probably thousands — of patterns of artificial fly which have been described in the fishing literature. Here we can do no more than introduce the various types of fly and their uses. A selection of typical and popular flies is given on the colour plates elsewhere in the book.

Flies for trout fishing can be divided into 'imitators' which are supposed to represent some recognised form of trout food and 'attractors', a name given to any fly which is known to take fish even though it would be difficult to pinpoint exactly what it represents.

Another major division is between dry flies (fished on the surface) and wet flies (fished beneath the surface). The Mayflies are an important group of imitators which can be fished wet or dry. Special patterns of lake flies have been developed to match the growth of interest in stillwater angling, while many flies have been particularly tied for catching salmon and sea-trout. A relatively modern innovation is the 'lure' type of flies, fished mostly in lakes and reservoirs, which are tied to represent many forms of aquatic life, from large nymphs to small fish.

In the rest of this chapter I have aimed to give enough of the basic principles of fly-tying to enable anyone to make a start at the hobby. The fly shown on the front cover of this book, the Wiggins Teape Conqueror, is a winged dry fly, and anybody who masters the craft of fly-tying to the stage where they can turn out a reasonable fly of this type is well on the way to being able to tie 'any fly in the book'.

TYING A HACKLED FLY

In all the instructions which follow, the fly-tyer is assumed to be sitting at his bench with the eye of the hook pointing to the right. 'To the rear' means towards the bend of the hook.

Waxing the tying silk. Draw off about 12″ of silk from the reel
pull it rapidly over a piece of fly-tying wax, keeping it in place
with a finger or thumb of the hand which holds the wax. The
movement should be very rapid so as to cause friction between the
wax and the silk. This melts the wax and coats it round the silk. A
slow movement will cause the silk to stick and will probably break
it.

Start winding silk about ⅛″ from the eye of the hook. Cut off the
tied-in end, and wind to a point on the shank where the bend
commences (figure 20*a*).

Tail. To make the tail take three of four fibres from a large stiff
hackle, usually of the same colour as that of the shoulder hackle.
The fibres should be about ¾″ to 1″ long, and are tied down on top of
the shank where the initial tying of silk ended. One turn of the silk
is enough, and then put another turn of silk under the tail close to
the previous one, and another turn round the shank in front of the
first one. This will give a smart lift to the tail of the fly (figure 20*b*).
The butt ends of the tail fibres can now be cut off, or left to form a
'bed' on which the body material can be wound.

Body. For the body we use a stripped quill from the 'eye' feather
of a Peacock's tail. Tie in the narrow end of the quill close to the tail
with two turns of silk, and then wind silk back to starting point
(figure 20*c*). Now wrap the quill round the shank towards the eye,
overlapping each turn very slightly. The bi-coloured quill will
then give a very good imitation of the rib markings found on many
flies. When the silk foundation has been covered, put two turns of
silk round quill and cut off surplus. We should now be as
figure 20*d*.

Hackle. For a dry fly a good stiff-fibred red cock's hackle should
be used, and for a wet fly a softer one or a hen's hackle. The length
of hackle to be used can be judged as follows: bend the hackle in the
middle, and the length of the fibres that will stand out should be
about the same as the distance between the eye and the point of the
hook.

Hold the hackle by the tip and strip off the soft fibres below the
dotted line (figure 20*e*). Draw the remaining fibres downwards so
that they stand out at right angles as in figure 20*f*. Now tie the
stripped butt under or on top of the hook shank near the eye
(figure 20*g*). The way the hackle is tied in is most important, so tie
it in the way you find most comfortable and convenient. I usually
hold it by the stem, on top of the shank, and fix it with a firm figure-
of-eight tying. I then bend the butt to the rear and take another
couple of turns round it, which brings the silk up to the body again.

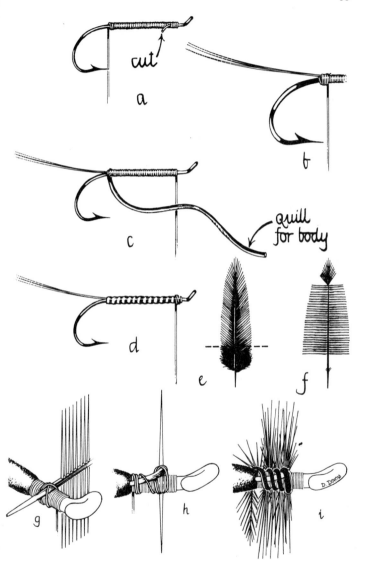

cut

quill
for body

a

b

c

d

e

f

g

h

i

D. Downe

20. *Tying a hackled fly* (see text)

Cut off surplus stem (figure 20*h*). The outside of the hackle should face the front and it is essential that it be tied in perfectly edgewise to the shank, otherwise the fibres will not stand out at right angles when the hackle is wound.

Now take the tip of the hackle in the hackle pliers and wind it three or four times clockwise to the rear (figure 20*i*). The turns should almost touch but never overlap. If they do the fibres will splay out and give a most unattractive appearance to the fly.

After the turns have been made, allow the tip of the hackle to hang down in hackle pliers, and wind a couple of turns of silk over it. Then cut off the tip of the hackle. Now wind silk through the hackle fibres towards the eye, binding down the hackle stem but avoiding the fibres. Make a whip finish when the silk is clear of the hackles as figure 21. To wind the silk through the hackle without binding down any of the fibres, keep the silk very taut, working it in between the fibres as you bind down the stem. Use a backwards and forwards motion, going further forward than back. Your finished fly should appear as one of the hackled flies shown in the colour plates, such as Tup's Indispensable.

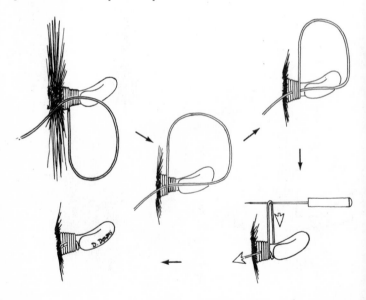

21. *The whip finish*

TYING A WINGED FLY

We can make a winged fly by merely adding a pair of wings to the hackled fly described in the previous section. This would produce a winged *dry* fly. By using a softer hackle, we can make a winged *wet* fly. The only difference is that on a wet fly the wings are tied as the last item of the dressing, whereas on a dry fly the wings are tied on before the hackle. We will deal with the wet fly first.

The fly is tied to the stage where the hackle is tied in, using a soft cock hackle, or an even softer hen's hackle. One must remember to leave enough room at the front of the body to take the wings as well as the hackle. After the hackle has been wound round the body, all the fibres should be drawn down underneath, and a turn of silk put over them to keep them in place as shown in figure 22. Note the space left at the front to take the wing, and the silk bed for it.

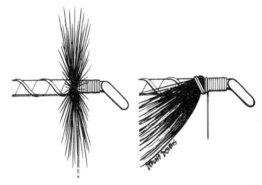

22. *Holding down the hackle fibres of a winged fly before applying the wing slips*

Before starting to tie a winged fly, a beginner would do well to practice the winging procedure on its own. To do this I advocate a largish hook, and a wing material consisting of fibres which stay together well. The best one I know is the primary feather from the wing of a wild duck (Mallard), and when one has mastered the simple technique which ensures that all the fibres of the material come down directly on top of the hook shank, winging becomes as easy as any other procedure. The following four points should be observed at all times:

(a) Grips the wings *and hook* tightly to ensure that the wing fibres come down vertically.

(*b*) Don't loosen the grip until at least three turns of silk have been drawn down firmly.

(*c*) If the wing splits, take it off and start again.

(*d*) Always ensure that the of silk is made first. Never tie wings on to a bare hook.

The natural shape of the feather fibres used for winging is utilised to give the desired shape to the wings themselves. If the top edge of the wing slips is at the top when the wings are tied in, the resulting wing will be as figure 23*a*. If put on upside down, the result is as figure 23*b*.

a   b

23. *Wing shapes obtained by tying in the wing slips with the top edge* (left) *and the bottom edge uppermost*

Select two roughly equal feathers as a pair, as shown in figure 24*a*, one feather from a left-hand wing, and another from a right-hand wing. Cut a slip from each as indicated. Figure 24*b* shows an exaggerated elevation drawing of part of a feather which illustrates the interlocking fibres on the wing 'herls' which we must utilise to keep our tied-in wings neat and tidy. The cross-section drawing illustrates the natural curve of the feather fibres on the quill, which we also utilise to give shape and style to our wet- and dry-fly wings.

Figure 24*c* shows a pair of wing slips offered to each other, curving inwards to make a wet-fly wing.

Figure 24*d* shows the wing slips held firmly between thumb and forefinger of the left hand — note how the thumb and forefinger envelope both wing and hook. The same figure shows the all important 'loop over the top' without which it is impossible to achieve a perfectly formed wing. The silk is brought up between the thumb and the feather, and then the weighted bobbin holder is used to slip the silk down on the other side between finger tip and feather. Figure 24*e* shows how the silk is drawn, still confined between the thumb and the forefinger, squeezing down the fibres one on top of the other. Figure 24*f* shows how, after two more turns of silk have been made in the same manner as for figure 24*d*, the silk can be kept taut by the weight of a bobbin holder while the waste ends of the wings are cut off, using scissors to make a side cut. These

89

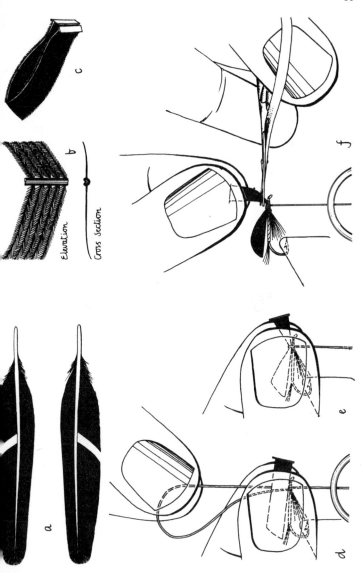

24. *Tying a winged fly* (see text)

ends (or butts) should taper slightly towards the eye. (This is
achieved by using the scissors flat so that they come down face-on to
the hook shank, and not edge-on.) Silk is then wound over the wing
butts and the fly is completed with a whip finish, ready after
varnishing, to go fishing.

The procedure for tying on dry-fly wings is exactly the same as
for wet-fly wings up to the stage where they are left horizontally on
top of the hook-shank (figure 24e), the main difference being that
the two wing slips are offered to each other so that their tips point
outwards instead of inwards. This is shown clearly in figure 25a.
The wings are then lifted into the vertical position and two or three
turns of the tying silk taken behind them, as shown in figure 25b.
Still holding the wings rigidly in the vertical position, another one
or two turns should be taken round at the extreme base of the slips
as in figure 25c. This will ensure that the wings stay in the upright
position. This part of the procedure is made easier if a bobbin
holder is used, as this can be 'thrown' to the rear of the fly with the
right hand, picked up again with the right hand, and wound round

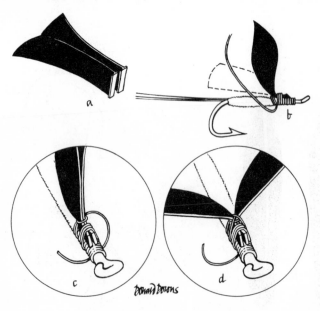

a

b

c

Donald Downs

d

25. *Tying on the wings of a dry fly*

the base of the wings. This is necessary as the left hand does not release its hold on the wing-tips during this part of the procedure. Finish off with a final turn round the hook-shank in front of the wings, also shown in figure 25c. The wings can now be released by the left hand and, if they do not spring apart of their own accord, use the point of the scissors or a dubbing needle to separate them.

What we do now is make a 'figure-of-eight' turn between the wings, as shown completed in figure 25d, and the fly is now ready for its hackle. It will be observed that a dry-fly hackle is put on after the wings, not before, as we did for the wet-fly. The finished fly should look like one of the winged dry flies shown on the colour plates, such as the Ginger Quill, or Greenwell's Glory.

HOW TO MAKE 'DUBBING' BODIES

Many patterns of fly specify fur bodies. These are made by winding 'dubbed' silk around the hook-shank. The process of dubbing basically consists of applying fibres of fur to the silk until it is encompassed completely, rather like the rubber casing around a piece of electric wire. Important points to remember during the spinning of the fur on the silk are:

(a) See that the tying silk is well waxed.
(b) Only use a small amount of fur at a time. Spread it out to cover as large an area of the thumb or finger as possible.
(c) Do not roll the silk backwards *and* forwards on the thumb, but in one direction only.
(d) Keep the tying silk taut all the time.

The procedure is as follows: hold the tying silk taut in the right hand, at right angles to the hook, pulling it towards the body. Select a minute pinch of fur and spread it on the ball of the left forefinger or thumb, whichever you find easiest. If it looks more like an almost indiscernible mist rather than a bunch of fur fibres, so much the better, especially for small trout flies. Now bring the taut silk down on the forefinger as figure 26a. Lower the thumb of the left hand on to the forefinger and roll the silk and the fur in a clockwise direction. This is the action which wraps the fur round the silk, and it should be repeated with additional fur until a sufficient length of the silk has been covered. Press the finger and thumb together firmly during the rolling, opening them at the end of each individual roll. I stress this point so that you will not keep the finger and thumb together and just roll the fur backwards and forwards. It will be obvious that if rolling in one direction wraps the fur round the silk, rolling it back again will tend to unwrap it!

The dubbing should now look like figure 26b, and is then wound towards the eye of the hook, not forgetting to leave enough space at the eye for any wings and hackles that have to be tied in. The spacing of the turns will regulate the thickness of the body, and they are usually overlapped at the shoulder of the fly so that extra thickness is given at this point (figure 26c). It is customary to give a tinsel rib of some sort to a dubbing body, and this is tied in at the tail before starting on the dubbing. By this method it is possible to make bodies light and translucent, or thick and shaggy, that will put up with an almost unlimited amount of use. If the latter type of body is required, say, for a salmon fly, it is still far better to apply only a little dubbing to the silk at a time, adding more until a good thick 'barrel' is achieved. Fibres can then be pulled out from this body with a dubbing needle to give the hackled effect often needed.

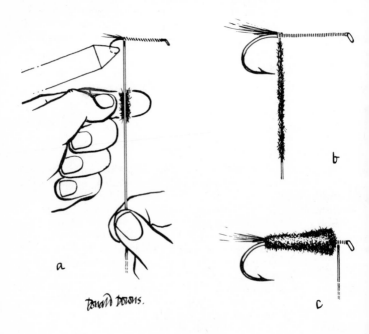

Donald Downs.

26. *Making a 'dubbing' body* (see text)

When using a fur which has to be cut from the skin before use, it should be cut so that the staple is as long as possible. If the fibres are cut off so that they are only about ⅛″ long, the difficulty of wrapping them around the silk is greatly increased. It is also a fact that some furs are more easily applied than others. Seal, for instance, is more difficult than rabbit or hare. This is due to the fibres of the seal's fur being stiffer and more springy than the others. The basic procedure is, however, exactly the same for all furs — it just means that the points I have emphasised must be more strictly observed with the difficult furs.

Another method should be noted which is particularly useful for those short-fibred dubbings which do not lend themselves easily to the spinning or rolling method I have described. The fly is formed to the stage where the dubbing is required, which would usually bring the tying silk to the tail. At this stage another piece of well-waxed tying silk is tied in, and some dubbing is placed between the two silks. They are then twisted together to embrace the dubbing, and wound round the hook to form the body, care being taken to see that the silks remain twisted together. Finish off with the original tying silk and cut off the end of second thread.

This brings me to a tip passed on to me by N. F. Bostock, an associate of the late G. E. M. Skues. Any thread which has a twist, as in this method, should be wound in the opposite direction to the twist. In other words, if the two silks which embrace the dubbing are twisted together anti-clockwise, they will not untwist when wound clockwise to form the body. This principle will also be found useful when bodies are being formed from floss silks which have a twist in them when taken from the reel. Winding them on in one direction will continue to twist the silk into a tight cord, whereas winding them on in the opposite direction will untwist them so that a flat, well-shaped body is achieved. A small point, but a timesaver.

MAKING NYMPHS

If a nymph is required without wing cases, all that is necessary is a hackled wet fly with a dubbing body much thicker at the shoulder or thorax so that a distinct hump is formed. Only one or two turns of the hackle for the legs should be used (figure 27a).

To tie a nymph with wing cases, let us consider a typical pattern, the March Brown Nymph. The materials required are listed overleaf.

HOOK: 12—14.

WING CASES: Woodcock wing feather.

TAIL: Three strands of brown mallard shoulder or brown partridge back feather.

RIB: Gold wire.

BODY: Darkish hare's fur from root of ears.

THORAX: As for body.

HACKLE: One turn of a small brown speckled partridge or grouse hackle.

Tie in a very small hackle for the legs, and then wind tying silk to about one-third of the distance between the eye and the bend of the hook. Now tear off a strip of fibres from the woodcock wing feather and tie in as shown in figure 27b. The fibres should be stroked

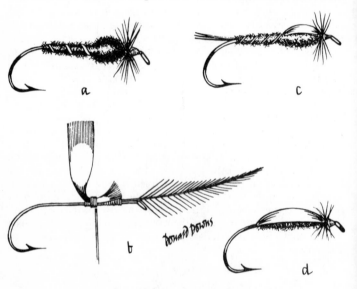

27. *Tying a March Brown Nymph* (see text)

towards the eye of the hook so as to be out of the way while the rest of the body is formed. Continue winding silk to the bend of the hook and tie in the tail and wire rib. Dub the fur on to the silk and wind it up to the wing cases. Now wind rib as far as the wing cases, tie it in and cut off the surplus. Dub more fur on to the silk and wind it in front of the wing cases to form the thorax. Now bring the wing cases down over the thorax, tie in and cut off the surplus. Wind one turn of the hackle cut off the tip, and finish off with a whip finish. The finished nymph should now be as figure 27*c*.

A very good method of making effective looking Mayfly nymphs, is to tie in the wing cases right at the bend of the hook, after the tail fibres have been fixed. The fur body is then wound on, and thickened at the front as described on page 92). The wing cases are then brought down and tied in at the front of the hook. The wire rib is now wound evenly, but fairly widely from the tail end, a large gap being left where the wing cases proper should hump up. The result is a very realistic looking segmented body.

For a beetle, the wing cases should be tied in at the bend of the hook so that they reach from the bend to the eye as figure 27*d*.

If nymphs or any other kind of wet flies are required to sink rapidly, a base of electrical fuse wire can be wound on first. This material is easier to use than the lead wire that is usually advocated.

A SHORT GLOSSARY OF FLY-TYING TERMS

BI-VISIBLE FLIES. These are designed to improve the visibility of flies to both angler and fish, particularly when using dark flies in poor light. It merely entails the adding of a white or light-coloured hackle to the front of the usual hackle. A white hackle wound in front of the hackle used on the Red Palmer produces a Red Palmer Bi-visible.

DETACHED BODY. The body of an artificial fly, complete in itself, tied on to the hook shank, but separate from it.

DUBBING. *See* Fur Bodies.

DUBBING NEEDLE. Used to pick out fur fibres on a 'dubbed' body, to simulate legs, feelers, etc.

FLUE. *See* Herls.

FLUORESCENCE. Some fly-tying materials are now treated so as to have this property. Useful for dull days and heavy water conditions. It is not possible to get dark shades, such as black, only pastel shades of the primary colours, or variations of them. Manufactured fibres such as nylon react very well to this treatment, but natural materials such as hackles can be quite effective also.

FUR BODIES. These are formed by twisting or dubbing furs on to the tying silk, and then winding them round the hook-shank to form the body of the fly.

HACKLE. Feather wound round the hook-shank to represent the legs or wings of a fly.

HAIR BODIES. These are formed by using the stiffish body hairs of the common deer. They are spun on to form a 'hackle' which is then cut to any desired body shape. This method is used not only because bulky bodies can be made up, but also for the extremely good buoyancy of this type of body.

HERLS. Short fibres or 'flue' which stand out from individual feather fibres or quills. When these fibres or quills are wound round the hook-shank, the 'flue' stands out at right-angles, imparting a certain amount of translucence to the solid body. Peacock and ostrich tail feather fibres are the two best examples of herls, but fibres from wing quills and tail feathers of many other birds are also used, heron, condor, goose and swan being very popular.

IRONS. This is the old Scottish name for salmon-fly hooks and has now become general idiom for any type of hook.

LOW-WATER FLIES. Very lightly dressed salmon flies, the wing-tips of which are dressed well forward of the bend of the hook. They are used in summer or low-water conditions by means of the 'greased line' method, in which the fly does not sink very far below the surface.

MALLARD FEATHERS FOR WINGS. One often comes upon this term in the dressing of a fly, but as the mallard supplies so many feathers for wings, some difficulty may be experienced in deciding which one to choose. Below are listed some of the different types of mallard feathers, and some well-known flies in which they are used.

Bronze mallard shoulder feathers: Mallard and Claret and all the other Mallard series of flies. Connemara Black, Golden Olive, Fiery Brown, Thunder and Lightning, Blue Charm, and nearly all other salmon flies which have mixed wings. *Grey mallard flank feathers:* This is a grey speckled feather similar to teal flank, but with much lighter markings. It is used for John Spencer, Queen of Waters, Grizzly King, Professor, and as a substitute for teal and pintail feathers in many salmon flies. *Grey mallard quill feathers:* These are the wing primary feathers, and can be used for nearly any fly which calls for a grey wing, particularly in the larger sizes, i.e. Silver Saltoun, Wickham's Fancy, Blae and Black. *Blue/white tipped mallard quill feathers:* These also come from the wing, the blue part of the quill being used for one of the best known of all flies — the Butcher. Strips taken from the white tip of the feather are used for Heckham and Red, and all the others of the Heckham series, McGinty, Jock, and, in fact, any fly which has a wing with a white tip. This includes small and low-water salmon flies where a white-tipped turkey tail feather would be too large.

MARRIED FIBRES. Fibres taken from different feathers and then joined together to form one whole wing section. Used mainly for mixed and built-wing salmon flies.

PALMER FLY. Any fly which has the hackle wound from shoulder to tail. A fly so dressed is usually referred to as 'tied Palmer'.

PARACHUTE FLY. This term is used for flies with the hackle wound in a horizontal plane instead of round the hook-shank.

QUILL. *Body:* usually formed by one of the fibres from a peacock's tail, after the flue has been stripped from it. Strips cut from the centre quill of tail or wing quill feathers with a knife can also be used. *Wings:* when a dressing calls for a wing from a 'quill', this means that the feather fibres from the quill are used for the wing.

RIBS. These can be formed of silk, herls or tinsels. On trout flies they are usually meant to simulate the segmentations of insect bodies, whereas on

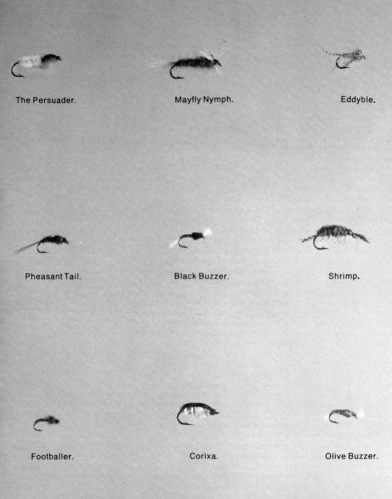

The Persuader.

Mayfly Nymph.

Eddyble.

Pheasant Tail.

Black Buzzer.

Shrimp.

Footballer.

Corixa.

Olive Buzzer.

Longhorns.

Baby Doll.

Large Pheasant Tail.

LURES

Sweeney Todd.

Orange Muddler.

Black Matuka (N.Z.).

Jersey Herd.

Black Lure (Tandem).

Polystickle.

Muddler Minnow.

Whisky.

Black Muddler.

Mylar Bodied Fly.

Black Marabou.

Church Fry.

salmon flies their function is to strengthen the body material and protect any body hackle if used.

SILK BODIES. Strands of silk, usually floss, wound directly on to the hook shank to form the body.

TAIL. *See* Whisks.

TAIL FEATHER. When a dressing calls for a wing or part of a wing from a tail feather, this means that the feather fibres from the tail are used. Grouse and Green uses feather fibres from the grouse tail.

TANDEM HOOKS. Two or more hooks whipped to gut, nylon monofilament, or wire, in line with each other. Used mostly for sea-trout and lake lures, sometimes referred to as Demons and Terrors. The now very popular Worm Fly is usually tied on a two-hook tandem.

TEAL FEATHERS FOR WINGS. As with the mallard, the teal supplies several feathers for wings. When a fly has a black-and-white barred feather for the wings, it is the breast or flank feather of the teal which is used. Such flies are Peter Ross, Teal and Green, Teal and Blue, and all the others of the Teal series. The grey feathers of the wing can be used for such patterns as Wickham's Fancy or any other largish pattern requiring a grey wing.

TINSEL. Strips of flat metal and strands of silk covered with metal. Used for whole bodies or just for ribbing. When in doubt use a flat tinsel for a whole body, and the covered silk tinsel for ribbing.

TINSEL BODIES. Bodies made of metal strip wound the length of the hook-shank, used to impart 'flash' to a fly, particularly those flies which are supposed to resemble a small fish.

TUBE FLIES. Flies which have the body hackle and wings (if any) tied on to a length of plastic or metal tubing. The hook is supplied by tying a double or treble hook to a length of gut, and passing it through the tube.

VARNISH. This is applied to the final turns or whip finish of the fly, to prevent the silk unravelling during use. Clear varnish is usually used for dry flies, while spirit and coloured varnishes are used for wet flies and salmon flies.

It is as well to have some method of ensuring that bottles of varnish are not knocked over whilst actually tying. A simple stand capable of taking a selection of varnishes and thinners can be made with cut-out holes to stand in the bottles and brushes.

WHIP FINISHER. A tool so designed to simplify the application of the whip finish of the fly. It is only suitable for this purpose and cannot apply whip finishes to rods, hooks to gut or any other article which has a projection beyond the actual whip finish.

WHISKS. Fibres of feathers used to form the tail. If material such as wool or silk is used, they are more often referred to as a 'tag' instead of a tail.

WINGS. Here is a list of the various types of wings used on trout and salmon flies: *Wet fly:* A flat wing sloping back over the body of the fly. *Double-split wing dry fly:* Formed of two sections each, taken from a pair of matched wing quills and tied in so that the tips point outwards. *Fan wings:* Formed of two small breast feathers, usually from the mallard drake, tied in to curve outwards. *Advanced wing:* Term used when the wing slopes over the eye of the fly instead of the body. Can be a flat wing or a double split wing. *Down wing:* Used for dry-flies which simulate the Sedge group, Stoneflies and Alder flies. *Rolled wing:* These consist of a roll of feather fibres taken from a wing quill or tail. They are used for the down-wing types mentioned above, and for some well-known types of North Country upright-winged dry flies. *Upright wing:* Any wing that stands upright from the body of the fly. They can be double-split wings, fan wings, rolled wings, hackle point wings, etc. *Bunch wings:* Wings formed by a bunch of fibres cut from any feather. They can be tied upright, low over the body, advanced or split. *Split wings:* Any wings that have their points separated. *Hackle point wings:* The tips of hackles are used to form the wings, two for most patterns, four for mayflies. *Spent wings:* Wings tied so that they lie flat on the water when the fly is cast, imitating the spent fly. Hackle points or hackle fibres are the most popular of this type. *Hackle fibre wings:* Similar to bunch wings in so far that a bunch of hackle fibres is used for the wings. *'Shaving brush' wings:* Hair or feather fibres tied in so that they point forward over the eye of the hook in line with the shank. Down-eyed hooks should be used to facilitate the tying on of the cast, or the tying silk should be so wound so as to form a slight split down the centre of the wing. *Streamer wings:* Wings formed of whole hackles or long strips of other feathers, the tips of which project well beyond the bend of the hook. *Strip wings:* Salmon-fly wings which are made of strips taken from one type of feather only. *Whole feather wings:* Term used when a whole feather or two whole feathers back to back, form the wing of the fly. *Mixed wings:* Wings that are formed from the fibres of several different feathers, 'married' together to form single whole sections. *Herl wings:* Wings that are formed with the feathers normally used for herl bodies. The Alexandra is the best-known example.

WING CASES. The hump incorporated in the dressings of nymphs and beetle imitations to simulate the wing housing. They are usually formed of feather fibres tied in at one point, folded down on to the body and then tied in at another point. If fur or silk is used for the body, this should be thickened between these two points so as to accentuate the hump.

Conrad Voss Bark

Stillwater Fishing

Stillwater fishing includes fishing on huge Irish loughs — rather like small inland seas — on the lochs and lochans of Scotland, which, as in Ireland, often contain sea-trout and salmon as well as wild brown trout; while in England and Wales, with a few exceptions, the fishing is mainly on artificially constructed lakes and reservoirs stocked with artificially bred fish, mostly the fast-growing American rainbow.

Lake and reservoir fishing, especially close to the large industrial areas of England, has developed enormously in the past 50 years to meet the needs of anglers. The rivers simply could not cope with the demand. So — because trout do not breed in still water — these waters had to be stocked with artificially bred fish, mainly rainbows, which are cheaper to produce and have a faster growth rate than brown trout.

In the last 25 years there has been a very rapid development of private lake fisheries, especially in England, which let out rods on a day ticket or subscription basis. In the natural lakes of Ireland and Scotland fishing for wild brown trout and sea-trout is still largely a matter of boat fishing — it is easier and more convenient — while in the reservoirs and small lakes in England and Wales the fishing is mainly fishing from the bank. English reservoir bank fishermen have developed techniques of fly fishing which are still largely unknown in Ireland and Scotland.

The principle of putting the fly to the trout is more or less the same on any lake but the methods vary enormously. So do the habits of the fish. Rainbows have some advantages because on the whole they are more resistant to disease and can stand higher water temperatures — therefore they are more likely to be found in shallow water than the browns in hot weather — but they also have a habit of schooling which means that sometimes they are difficult to find. Pound for pound the wild brown trout is a much more savage fighter than a rainbow from a put-and-take fishery and the sea-trout even more so. A 10 lb plus stewpond rainbow from an English put-and-take fishery is a very sluggish fish by comparison. The best fighting rainbow from these fisheries is generally from between 1 lb – 3 lb but the bigger fish are, of course, good publicity value.

Basically there are two methods of fishing for stillwater trout, whether one is fishing an Irish lough or an English reservoir. The first is to fish a lure — a fly which is intended to stimulate the trout to take hold of it even though it doesn't *necessarily* represent any known insect — and the second is to fish a fly which is intended to represent or suggest one of the natural food forms in the lake on which the trout lives.

Both these methods are used, and sometimes overlap, in all fishing on still waters, whether from the bank or from a boat, and we will deal with them in sequence, first of all with bank fishing with floating and sunk lines, and then boat fishing.

BANK FISHING

The Floating Line: Lures
The floating line can be used to fish attractor patterns of flies (lures) as well as deceiver patterns (imitations or suggestions of the natural insect) both on the surface of the water, in the surface film, and down to a depth of perhaps 8 to 10 ft.

Most reservoir fishermen use a shooting head or a weight-forward line, especially for lure fishing, so that they can cast further and cover larger areas of water. For smaller waters and for fishing deceiver patterns an ordinary double-taper line is sufficient. Most beginners start by fishing a lure and to do that you have to be able to cast reasonably well and put your fly out 15" – 20 yards or even further.

Whenever you go to a reservoir, there is always the problem: what fly do you use? Frankly, when lure fishing, it does not matter very much what pattern you fish from among the several thousand patterns that are available. A pattern you like the look of or a friend has recommended is good enough to begin with. But one thing is important. If the water is rough you want to use a fairly heavy fly, say a Jersey Herd, size 8 or 6. If it is smooth then use a smaller and lighter fly, say a Butcher or Peter Ross, size 10 or 12.

Attach your fly — a tucked blood-knot is the most commonly used knot — to an ungreased leader about 9 ft long. If you are fishing a big lure deep and fast on waters where there are big trout the point of your leader ought to be of a breaking strain of between 5 and 8 lbs. If you fish a smaller lure slowly, close to the surface, then the leader point might be between 3 and 5 lbs.

Where do you fish? If the fish are showing, that is a good guide to where they are. If not then you might just as well start not too far away from other anglers. If one of them catches a fish it will give you confidence. If they are standing in the water — in some lakes wading is not permitted — then wade in at the end of the line some 30 yards away from the end man. Don't push in between anglers already in position. Wade quietly. Don't create waves. Don't splash.

Then it is a matter of casting out your lure a reasonable distance and, after allowing it to sink, pulling line back in with your left hand, the non-casting hand, while keeping the line crooked round the first finger of the hand holding the butt of the rod. The loose line is allowed to fall on the water or, sometimes, if you are using a shooting head, into a line-tray attached to your waist.

Bring your lure in as far as you can and make sure a fish is not following it before you begin another cast. If you whip the line from the water just as a fish takes, a break is almost certain.

Now vary your retrieve, both the speed and the depth at which the lure is fishing. Sometimes let it sink deep and strip it in fast, sometimes fish it shallow, both fast and slow, sometimes jerking it in, sometimes bringing it in smoothly. You never know, until you try, what kind of a movement will attract the fish. Some men use very long leaders — 12 ft or more — and even nip a small split shot just in front of the eye of the hook to make it sink deeper faster. A beginner ought to avoid using split shot because it does make casting *slightly* more difficult. But if the fish are lying deep it certainly helps to get down to them.

When fishing a lure do make sure that the rod makes an angle to the line of retrieve. This helps to cushion the shock of a hard take. If the lure is deep and the leader completely sunk the trout will very often hook himself and the first you will know of it will be a bang on the rod. A lure fished fairly slowly close to the surface is often taken just as hard but then the swirl of a take and the whipping away of the nylon does give a moment's warning. A quick lift of the rod — not a strike — and the fish should be hooked.

This method of fishing sounds simple — not very different from using a spinner — and indeed it is. But the fact is that some lure fishermen consistently catch more fish than others. They study the water. They explore and seek out the shoaling rainbows while others stay in the same place and just go on flogging the water. They develop their own methods of the retrieve. They seek out sunken weed beds, deep gullies, any place where they suspect trout are likely to be. If they see a trout hunting small fry then they put up a fishlike lure — a Polystickle, for example — and make it sink and waggle and wallow in the water like a wounded fish. There are many ways in which a good lure fishermen can tempt a trout.

And, of course, a good lure fisherman will not only use the attractor patterns of fly all the time. When appropriate, he will — as we say — fish the natural, that is the deceiver patterns, flies that imitate or suggest the trout's natural food.

The Floating Line: 'Fishing the Natural'

There are several *hundred* different kinds of creatures that trout feed on underwater. Shrimps, water snails, and the nymphs and pupae of water-bred flies are among the most common. Sometimes the trout feed on them at random. Sometimes, if one particular insect is available in large quantities they will feed on these for a time almost to the exclusion of all others.

The principle of fishing the natural is to present a fly that suggests or represents the natural insect to trout which are feeding or are likely to feed on that particularlar kind of insect. But do not imagine you need to be an entomologist to fish the natural. It does help (and it adds a great deal of interest) if you know something about the insect life of lakes but if you do not you can still fish a general pattern which suggests some or even many of the most common forms.

A very good pattern to begin with is the Black Spider, which has been a popular lake pattern for more than a century, or variations on this, such as the Black and Peacock Spider. It gives the impression of a snail or pupa — there are millions of these in any sizeable lake — as well as a number of other creatures. Fish this very slowly indeed. It should be 'inched in' as we call it. You pull it in very gently, using only your fingers, just occasionally giving it a twitch. You are trying to imitate the movements of a living thing. They don't tear about the lake in top gear. Sometimes they move a few inches in short jerks. Very often they move very slowly. So the natural must be fished very slowly. It may take five minutes or even longer to fish out a 20-yard cast.

If there is a hatch of 'buzzers', and dark flies with crooked bodies are seen flying over the lake, trout take the pupae from which they hatch from the surface film in great numbers. A Black Spider or a midge pupae pattern can then be fished on the end of a greased cast, allowed to drift and, occasionally, twitched.

Other flies you are likely to see are olives and sedges. Both these hatch from insects rising to the surface — the olive nymph and the sedge pupa. If you fish the artificial nymph or pupa then let them sink, draw them slowly upwards, and allow them to sink again — a

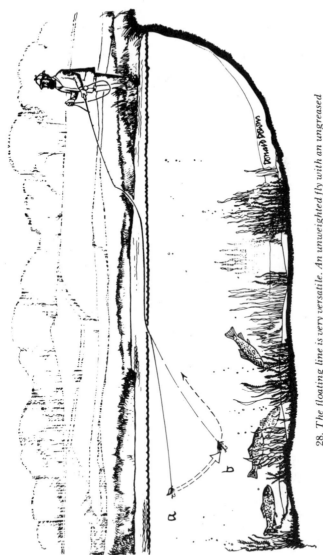

28. *The floating line is very versatile. An unweighted fly with an ungreased leader would normally fish in about position a. A weighted fly normally goes down to about position b, and with a really long leader deeper still*

slow sink-and-draw motion.

But many other insects can also be imitated including water boatmen (Corixae), shrimps, water lice, and so on, so that amid so much choice of patterns the beginner is likely to become confused. When in doubt, and until more knowledge is absorbed about underwater life, it is best to stick to a few simple patterns such as the spider and various sizes of nymphs (hooks 10—14) in brown and olive colourings. The Gold-ribbed Hare's Ear is a good general pattern of nymph and so are the various Ivens' nymphs and the Sawyer bugs.

If the lake is *very* clear you can sometimes see trout cruising along under the surface. Cast your nymph or spider in front of a cruising fish, wait until he comes near, then give it a slight movement. Watch him and if he opens his mouth or diverts slightly from his path tighten at once. This type of fishing is enormously exciting but — alas! — you do need gin-clear water to see what is happening.

Nymph fishing is an art in itself and some anglers become so fascinated by it that they fish nothing else. It is very delicate fishing and needs considerable concentration. One reason for this is that when a trout takes a nymph or a spider pattern, fished as they should be, very slowly or almost stationary, it does so gently. All you see is a slight twitch of your line on the surface or perhaps the butt of the nylon leader sliding away from you over the water. Sometimes you see nothing at all but a slight stoppage of the leader. If you do, tighten at once in order to set the hook while it is still in the trout's mouth. If not, the next second the nymph will be ejected by the trout as uneatable and you will not hook him.

When fishing the nymph, point your rod directly at the spot where the nymph is and keep the rod point low on the water. When you see the slight movement of the nylon or line that indicates a take, lift your rod point and *feel* for the fish. If your sight is poor or there is a glare or heavy ripple on the water whip a piece of wool on the end of your line. It acts like a float — a bite indicator.

The Floating Line: Dry Flies

A fly fished floating on the surface of the water can, at times, be very deadly. No one quite knows why. Very few winged flies are found in the stomachs of lake trout — most of their food is sub-aqueous — and yet they will often rise to a dry fly. Sometimes they will take a size 12 Black Palmer floated on the surface while they are actually feeding on midge pupae hanging in the surface film. But one of the best times to fish a floating fly is during an evening rise to

Sedge flies. Some of the Sedges have a habit of scuttling over the water after hatching. A bushy Red Palmer size 12 or 10, tweaked across the surface in little jerks, is often taken with a slashing rise. Fish these flies with a strong leader point. I use Palmer flies for surface fishing because they float well but of course there are excellent winged patterns of most of the well-known Sedge flies.

During the day, if there are any Olives about, a size 12 Greenwell will often rise a fish.

When a trout takes on the surface don't strike immediately you see the rise because you may well pull the fly out of his mouth. Give him a chance to close his mouth and put his nose down before you tighten and you will have a better chance of setting the hook.

When fishing the dry fly make sure that most of your cast, apart from the point, is greased well and that the fly itself is well soaked in a good floatant. Cast your fly to a rise, dropping it as near as you can to the rings, and let it drift. Twitch it a little from time to time. When it has drifted out of that area retrieve it slowly and cast again to the same place. If it appears unhopeful try a smaller fly, and a finer point on your leader. One expert dry-fly fisherman on lakes that I know uses 2 lb breaking strain nylon on the point of his leader and fishes flies as small as 16 and 18. With this equipment he takes rainbows averaging over 2 lbs in weight. As you can imagine, he has a delicate touch.

As with nymph fishing, keep your rod point low and pointed towards the fly. Lift the rod gently to set the hook. In that way you ought to be able to avoid a break.

On the whole, you are not likely to take many trout on the dry fly at the opening of the season when the air is cold and there is not much fly life about. Nor are you likely to take them in a heatwave in water that is approaching 70 °F. But, having said that, if you do see a rise then the possibility of a surface fly shouldn't be left unexplored. To see your fly disappear in a rise is tremendously exciting. You have to discipline yourself, in advance, not to strike too soon.

The Sunk Line

If it is cold in early spring or very hot in midsummer, if there is a vast expanse of tumbled water and big waves, with not a rise to be seen, then the likelihood is that the trout are lying and feeding deep. In fact, as a generalisation, it is true to say that most trout for most of the time do feed deep. If they are feeding in the shallows they can be caught with a fly on a floating line, but if they are deeper than about 8 ft then you have to use a sunk line to get down to them.

For most bank fishing a slow or medium slow sinking line is about right. Some fishermen carry two rods, one fitted with a floating and the other with a sinking line, but for those — like myself — who don't like to carry two rods one will do. Carry a separate reel with a sinking line on it, or on a spare spool for your reel. It doesn't take long to change over.

Figure 29 shows how the sunk line takes the fly down to the weed-grubbing trout. In fishing the sunk line it is best to use a buoyant fly, so that the fly floats, hopefully, above the weed, and doesn't get snagged. There are also special non-snag flies tied on keel hooks which float upside down with the point uppermost.

If you want your fly to scrape the bottom then use a short leader, no more than 5 to 6 ft long. But — and this is terribly important — use a much stronger leader in sunk-line fishing than in sub-surface fishing. When I fish a sunk line I use a leader with an 8 lb point and if I fished a lure fast I would use a 10 lb point.

When a big trout takes he can sometimes take quite savagely, especially if you're fishing a lure, and he also takes against the pressure and drag of the whole of that part of the line which is under water. He can run you out 80 yards or more into the lake and go very deep indeed. That's why quite a lot of sunk-line fishermen use shooting heads. The pressure on the nylon monofilament backing is much less than the pressure on 30 yards of sunk line, plus the ordinary backing.

Now, *how* do you fish a sunk line?

If you can't see any deep weed beds to explore, and often you can't, you search the water. You are a hunter. You seek your fish out. If you are fishing in company with a row of other fishermen on both sides of you then you haven't much choice. You wade in and cast as far out as possible. Then you'll probably feel the need for a shooting head.

If you like fishing well away from a crowd you will have a better chance to try different techniques. The fact that a lot of fishermen happen to be fishing in one particular place doesn't necessarily mean that is where all the trout are. Very often fishermen group together because that part of the water happens to be near the car park or the angler's hut! So do not hesitate to be different and get away on your own. You may well find a school of rainbow for yourself.

Find a promontory somewhere where you can cover fairly deep water and fish all round, fanning out your casts, starting with short casts to begin with and then reaching out. Try different speeds of retrieve. Fish your fly at different levels. Change the size and pattern

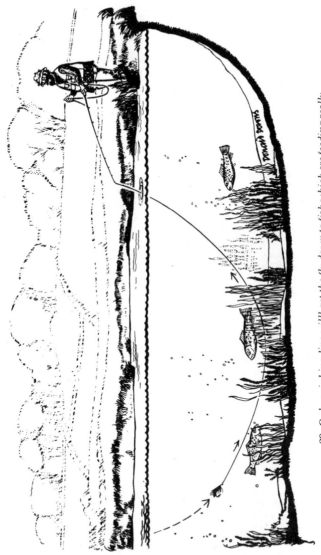

29. Only a sinking line will get the fly down to fish which are feeding really deep — say more than 8—10 ft below the surface. A buoyant fly on a sinking line is useful as it helps to prevent snagging in the weeds

of your fly. Experiment and go on experimenting. Never, never never be content to cast your fly out and keep on stripping it in at the same speed. For one thing it is not good fishing and for another it can get boring.

If the fish are very dour there are so many things you can do to tempt them. One very hot day at Blagdon when most sunk-line men were using large lures one man put on a small Black Palmer, a size 14, and fished it slowly, very slowly, and deep, close to the dam. He got his limit when nobody else was taking a fish. Another man I met at Weir Wood had taken his limit with a very primitive fly, a thin thread of red wool, whipped on to the shank of a bare hook just by the eye. It imitated a Bloodworm and he fished it very slowly indeed close to the bottom.

When fishing a fly on a sunk line you will feel rather than see the take. A fish taking a fly fished on a sunk line takes it *against* the drag and pressure of the line in the water and this is sufficient to set the hook. Therefore, fish with your rod at an angle to the retrieve. The spring of the rod takes up the pressure from a hooked fish. There will be a sudden bang and the trout will be on.

If you feel a sharp pluck at your fly and nothing else it is possible that the trout has tweaked but not taken. Change to a smaller fly and try him again, fished a little slower.

What are the best flies for sunkline fishing — lures or naturals?

Most of the really big fish that are taken near or close to the bottom, or weed beds, are generally taken on flies that either imitate or suggest natural food forms. The Worm Fly is not unlike some of the big larvae or beetles and the Muddler suggests these too. The Muddler is also very buoyant and not easily snagged. There are many good patterns of Sedge pupae, Nymphs, Shrimp and Midge pupae you can try.

Remember there are hundreds of underwater bugs you *can* imitate and the trout are used to seeing most of them, so that in sunkline fishing you don't have to worry quite so much about selective feeding as you do when surface fishing to say, a hatch of midge.

Trout eat great numbers of comparatively small insects so a size 10 hook is about right for sunk-line work. You can go up or down a few sizes but don't go too small, partly because the hook may not take hold properly and partly because smaller hooks are more likely to break through weaknesses in the metal.

Lures do take trout, and very big trout, in sunk-line fishing but on the whole you will probably stand a better chance of a fish if you mount a fly that at least suggests one of the natural food forms on which the trout lives.

One important thing to remember is always bring your sunk line gently to the surface before trying to cast out again. Dragging a sunk line out of deep water with too much force can easily damage or even break a rod. In this, as in everything else, all the best fishermen have a delicate touch.

BOAT FISHING

The Floating Line

Boat fishing is, possibly, the oldest form of stillwater fishing there is. It has been practised in Irish loughs and Scottish lochs for generations. There are many variations and refinements. The traditional way is for two anglers to share a boat, one in the bows and the other in the stern. They use longish rods, about 10 ft, and a point fly and a 'dropper' on the leader.

The boat is rowed upwind by the ghillie who then turns it sideways on and allows it to drift downwind, lending a hand with an oar now and again to turn it into likely places. The anglers cast their flies in the direction of the drift, with the wind behind them, and the flies are worked back towards the boat. The aim is to keep the point fly under the surface while the dropper bounces along on the surface, through and over the crests of the waves.

In Scotland rather brightly coloured flies are used — the Butcher and the Peter Ross are good examples — but in Ireland the tradition is to use darker and more natural coloured flies, suggestions of Mayflies, and of midges, which in Ireland are called duck-flies. In many of the lakes which have access to the sea there are sea-trout and salmon as well as brown trout. If you hook a 5 lb sea-trout — in Ireland called white trout — on a fine leader point you are in for the fight of your life.

In some Irish loughs dapping for trout with live Mayflies impaled on a hook is still practised but often a big bushy artificial is used instead. The angler uses a 14—16 ft rod and a very light floss silk line which blows out in front of him on the wind. The fly is so manoeuvred that it dances and bobs on the waves — a kind of dancing dry fly. When a trout leaps at it and takes the angler counts up to four or five before tightening. Crane flies — both real and artificial — are also used for dapping when they are on the water.

Fishing the drift does need a good ripple to be effective. In a dead calm you get out the whisky and put your feet up and go to sleep!

On English and Welsh reservoirs fishing the drift is sometimes possible, if there are boats, and in one or two reservoirs it is apparently becoming more popular. But ghillies are few and far between so that either outboard motors are used or one of the anglers rows up to the start of the drift. Then a drogue is put over the side (see figure 30) to slow down the drift and both anglers fish, casting in front and retrieving or else casting to each side and letting the flies swing round as the boat moves past.

30. *A simple form of drogue for slowing down the rate of drift of a boat. It consists of a canvas square with a small hole in the centre, corded at four corners, and roped by the hole so that it can be reversed and brought on board when necessary. The angler is very wisely wearing soft shoes*

One of the most important things to remember in boat fishing is that every year there are accidents, some of them fatal. It is dangerous to stand up or change places. Keep seated and do not wear waders. Rubber-soled shoes are best. If your watch is not waterproof leave it with your wallet, locked in the car. If you do capsize, conserve your energy, hang on to the boat and wait for help or for the boat to drift into the shallows. And another important thing is to remember that out on a big lake it can be very cold and very wet indeed. You need warm and very waterproof clothing, including a pair of waterproof trousers and a thick and springy cushion to sit on. Several hours sitting on a wooden seat can be hell.

The direction of the drift depends, of course, on the direction of the wind. It is one of the traditions of boat fishing that the best fish are often taken when fishing *towards* the bank. Sometimes this is so, and sometimes not — like so much else in fishing — but if there are anglers on the bank remember that the water within reach of their casts is theirs, not yours.

Some of the most productive water to explore from a boat is where shallow water suddenly dips into a deep hollow, around islands, near the run-in of streams, along the calm lanes between patches of rippled water, and, of course, any area where the fish are seen to rise.

The Sunk Line

In most boat fishing a sunk line is a handicap because of the strain of pulling it out of the water — but when the boat is anchored instead of being allowed to drift then it becomes, in effect, a casting platform, and the sunk line comes into its own. This technique is sometimes used on some of the bigger reservoirs in the Midlands. Lead-cored sinking lines — for these you need very strong rods — take the fly down very quickly to depths of 40—50 ft or more. Shooting heads are used to lessen line resistance and gain a good distance. Very big flies are generally the rule — large attractor patterns like a Black Lure — but sometimes one or even several deceiver patterns are fished on a very strong leader with droppers.

There have been few reports as yet of sunk-line fishing from boats in the big lakes in Ireland and Scotland but the possibility of catching one of the huge wild brown trout of Loch Awe, for example, might well be increased considerably by the use of a deeply sunk lure. It is a comparatively new method of boat fishing and well worth exploring.

SEA AND SEA-POOL FISHING

The Floating Line

Sea pools are hardly still waters but they are, nevertheless, pools, so they are worth a mention. Brown trout as well as sea-trout can be taken on the fly in many sea pools at the mouth of rivers, especially in Ireland and Scotland. I have caught numbers of small brown trout in the sea pools of the Western Isles on the dry fly. They were most beautifully marked and as yellow as butter.

It is well worth remembering to take a fly rod along with you on a seaside holiday. You should not have too much trouble from the corroding effects of salt water if you always rinse the rod and reel and line very thoroughly in clean, fresh water after fishing. But take a fibre-glass or carbon-fibre rod rather than your best split cane.

Fish a sea pool when the tide is at the flood — or perhaps for an hour or so each side of high tide, depending on conditions. You will normally have to use a fairly large and heavy wet fly — a streamer or bucktail pattern — which you fish down and across the direction of the current. Let it swing round and bring it in slowly, making it look as though it is fighting against the tide, like a small fish or sand-eel.

If the water is clear you may well see a trout suddenly shoot up out of a patch of seaweed and drag your fly down. If nothing happens in the sea pool itself try further down towards the breakers. It is exciting fishing because you never know what will happen next, or what kind of fish will rise to you. Bass, pollack, mackerel, and small codling, or billet, all take a fly. Many of the possibilities of fly fishing in sea pools, and at sea, have still to be explored.

LANDING A FISH

Do not try and check the first frantic run of a big reservoir trout. Hold your rod point well up and let him tire himself against the spring of the rod. Only when he is really tired, on the surface, and has turned on his side, can you slide him towards you over the water.

Have a big landing net and sink it deep. Then slide him over the net and lift it to trap him. The rod arm goes back, the fish slides in, the net comes up. That is how it happens in theory. In practice he will probably see you, panic, start kicking, or take off for the horizon. Be prepared.

If a rainbow makes a long run and is going deep into weed put on side-strain by altering the angle of the rod to one side. This may throw him off balance. If he gets into weed, slack off strain and wait a minute, two minutes, five minutes. He may come out. If he does not try hand-lining him in. If that does not work wait and do nothing for some time. Try again. If you are irretrievably snagged then you have to break by pulling the line with your hand *not* with the rod.

Unless you are using an automatic reel (*see* p. 38), you will probably find that you will not be able to wind in fast enough, especially if the fish runs towards you, as they often do. In that case, strip in line fast with the hand that is not holding the rod. Keep up a steady pressure *all* the time whether you are holding the line by hand or playing him off the reel.

In river fishing, keep downstream of your fish if you possibly can while playing him. When exhausted he will drift downstream with the current. Let him drift into the net.

Do not snatch at the fish with the net. Keep up a firm pressure and wait for the spring of the rod to tire him out. Then *lead* him into the net, firmly but gently.

To kill a fish you use a 'priest' — the fisherman's name for a weighted stick that provides the last rites. Kill him quickly by hitting him on the back of the head just above and slightly behind the eyes. Do not bash him with a stone or hit his head on a rock. He will of course die naturally after some time out of water. Fishermen generally accept that it causes less suffering if he dies quickly.

On some lakes you can return undersize fish. Abide by the rules on this. If you are returning the fish sometimes you can hold the hook and he will kick himself off. If you have to handle him put your hands in water first. It causes him less pain. If he bleeds, kill him, because that may mean he is too damaged by deep hooking to survive. Some anglers, by the way, especially in America, are now using barbless hooks. They are well worth trying but beginners may lose a few fish through a slack line.

Wilson Stephens

Fishing Rivers and Streams

Fishermen talk of salmon rivers and trout streams. The distinction
goes beyond size. It includes the realisation, soon to dawn on all
who fish with a fly, that a river consists of a series of interplaying
streams. They combine like the filaments which form a rope, yet
remain distinct from each other, even though at first glance the
river continues to look like a single moving mass of water.

To a salmon, the area of manoeuvre is the whole river; a trout or a
grayling more commonly confines its movements to a component
stream of the river in which it has taken station, and which it knows
intimately. Recognition of this is the first step in 'reading the
water', a phrase which will recur as this chapter proceeds. This skill
forms the basis of all fly-fishing tactics and techniques; without it
all else is reduced to the level of guessing the lucky number at
roulette.

Most fish are caught because the fisherman has read the water
accurately, and correctly judged the proper way and the proper
place for using his tackle; some fish are caught by sheer fluke; there
is no middle way. He who trusts to fluke, and most men begin by
doing this, does so because he has omitted to learn the basics of his
sport. These words are carefully chosen; he must learn the basics for
himself by the observation of nature in the form of fish, fly, water
and weather. No other man can teach him if he does not seek to
know. This chapter gives guidance on how to observe and how to
deduce. It cannot do more.

It is sensible to approach the basics from the standpoint of trout
fishing. The trout is the fly fisherman's prototype quarry. There is
nothing in fishing for salmon, sea-trout or grayling which is not a
modification of the fundamental processes of trout fishing, from
which it will be possible to digress when necessary.

No two moving waters are identical. The longer a man fishes the
more clearly he sees that few are even similar, except in the broadest
sense. Points of origin and the environment through which they
flow give all rivers and streams separate identities. Imagination
will reveal how this comes about.

At first waterways were accidents of nature. As the millennia passed each developed its own character — geological, vegetational, meteorological, eventually ecological — so that now the flowing water has shaped the landscape by gouging out and draining its valley, providing a focus for all creatures, some of which live wholly or partly in it. The water and the land through which a river flows are interdependent, and a different species of river emerges from every combination. Long rivers rising in granite mountains distant from the sea· will be acid in content, peat-stained, broad flowing from their fairly constant water supplies; the Tay in Scotland, the Lune in England are examples. Short rivers of similar origin, because they fall more steeply, vary from headlong spates to narrow trickles — for instance the Glaslyn in Wales, the Orchy in Scotland. Those which rise in and flow over limestone (such as Usk and Dove) are 'grey water' rivers, first class for trout. Obvious differences distinguish the rain-fed streams of the Welsh Borders and elsewhere, which rise and fall as storms pass, from the chalk streams of Wessex and East Yorkshire. The latter are in fact springs emerging from deep underground aquifers in which water gathers after being filtered through the chalk. Months elapse between its fall as rain and its emergence as, say, the Test, Itchen or Driffield Beck the flows of which are unaffected by the immediate weather.

Within these categories the contrasts are limitless. Rivers have their character, even their personalities. To fish a new river, especially if wading, is like riding an unfamiliar horse. It is necessary to gain insight to it, to understand and predict it, to build a rapport with it, even to love it. Those who do not find the last-mentioned within their power ought not to be fishing.

This dissertation may seem remote from the act of fishing. Its purpose is to point the truth that there can be no single code of practice for flyfishing unless the fisherman himself can modify not only his methods but also his mood. Between the extremes of spring on the upper Wye, where the weight of the river's clutch on one's waders can have the force of a rugby tackle, and summer on the Lambourn, a stream as secretive as a maiden, there are innumerable gradations. The Wye throws down a challenge; the Lambourn is to be wooed; the man who cannot sensitise himself to such needs will not make a happy flyfisher.

On the practical level the characteristics of a river determine the style in which it is best fished. Consider the three methods normally employed for trout, and the conditions on a water which make each of them most effective.

THE UPSTREAM DRY FLY

We consider this method first, because it has been more discussed than any other. It confers on the fisherman the advantage of being able to see, as distinct from merely feeling, what happens. The fly is cast either to a visible fish, or to a point in the water where a fish has been seen to rise. It then floats, and hence is visible, until something or nothing happens. If it is taken it can be seen to be sucked under, or to disappear into the neb of the rising fish. The fisherman can then hook and play his trout (*see* p. 112) over a part of the river bed which he has been able to see throughout the time in which he has been casting for that particular fish.

31. The tactical problem. (a) *A good trout has been seen and stalked.* (b) *Several smaller fish, interposed, will scare off the target fish by stampeding upstream if the fisherman scares them. He must find a position from which to cast which offers best change of the line falling outside the field of vision of any of the small fish, and least chance of encountering drag. The fall of the line indicates the theoretical best approach — which is fine on a windless day, for those who cast well enough, and have luck on their side!*

For the dry fly to be effective the prime requirement is the visibility of the fish or its rise-form. If the water is too rough, or too thick and the fish feeding too deep in it for the fisherman to see his target, he should choose another method. But if the visibility is good enough, he has advantages not obtainable in any other way, and only one source of difficulty.

It is true to say that the dry fly demands perfect casting (or within five per cent of perfection), careful forethought, and skill largely borne by experience in approaching the target fish. In all other respects it is the easiest form of flyfishing because the fisherman knows so much that the element of surprise is much reduced and may be totally eliminated. This comforting thought has been often obscured since the definitive writings on the method were published by F. M. Halford near the turn of the last century. A certain stateliness of style and rigidity of reference spread the impressions that the dry fly in some way possessed moral virtues, could be successfully employed only by persons of quite exceptional talent, and even that it demanded a certain social status.

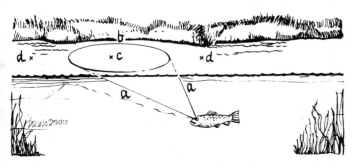

32. What the trout sees. (a) *A fish's field of view is roughly a 45° cone.* (b) *Because a feeding fish looks forward and up, not directly up, this represents an oval field of view at surface.* (c) *A fly floating within this oval is visible, whether or not it is taken.* (d) *Flies falling outside it are not visible, so will not be taken, however desirable.* Not correct !

This was not what he intended, nor is it true. He had propagated the code of the dry fly as an easier way, not a more respectable way, to catch trout in the particular circumstances of a chalk stream (in his case the Test). His stipulation of 'upstream' was not made out of subservience to some mythical code of decency, but because there is nothing to be gained and almost everything to be lost by fishing the dry fly downstream — the surface bow wave created by a dry fly held back against the current by an angler's line is enough to put down any sane trout. Halford accepted, as does everybody else, that all field sports are for gentlemen of all classes, and that in none of them is this quality more obvious than in the companionship of flyfishers of all kinds, whether on or off the river. In short, the dry fly is a practical measure, not an ethical distinction.

THE WET FLY

The man who begins his career as a fly fisherman on a dry-fly water is likely to be an exception. He is also, in the writer's opinion, less fortunate. While mastery of the dry fly confers ability to catch trout in specialised, though very attractive surroundings, it is mastery of the wet fly which is fundamental to all game fishing. Erroneously it is regarded as elementary, the beginner's method, the duffer's consolation, a sub-stratum of the sport about which the sophisticated may be patronising. The truth may perhaps be put in this way: the beginner will learn to catch fish more quickly, and with less frustration by this method than by any other. He will probably find such fishing more easily and at less cost than any other. And to become first-class at it he will need to learn more, to think more, and to sink more of himself in nature than with any other.

It is one thing to fish for a day and end it with two or three trout, as is possible for a wet-fly man whose experience can be counted in hours. Let none despise such an occasion; success in flyfishing is always sweet; a day on wet-fly water cannot be other than memorable; these are rewards in themselves. But it is another thing to share a day with a polished exponent of the downstream wet-fly, and to see how far removed it is from the chuck-it-and-chance-it image which some give it. Disdaining the athleticism of the long cast, such a man will produce fish by skill and accuracy which others would have left unsuspected, purely by skill at reading the water.

The basis of wet-fly fishing is not the visible evidence of the dry-fly technique, but well-founded suspicion. Ten yards of a brook may well contain all the physical components of a salmon pool with lies, taking places, dead water interspersed and trout positioned as salmon would be. In such a place the man who can relate the surface of the stream to the geography of its bed will shortly enjoy a dish of trout. And when he wades into Spey or Dee, or fishes from a boat on the broad waters of Tweed, he will not need his ghillie to tell him where to cast. He will have learned it already.

A salmon river is daunting by its sheer size, not to mention its prestige. No man surveying the immensity of the water rolling towards him and, more importantly, rolling away, can analyse its anatomy at a glance without enough practice to give him instinctive understanding. Practice is best had on wet-fly trout water. There, yard by yard, the topography of the bed and the interplay of currents are of minute-to-minute concern. The fisherman tunes himself into them. They become knitted to his reflexes as surely as does the boil of a fish as it takes.

In estimating wet-fly fishing there is a further consideration, less practical but not less valuable. This is a sport of small waters, and of lively waters. As they swing between meadows on the Welsh March, thread the combes of the West Country moors, dance through the grey and green of Pennine dales, or leap chamois-like down Scottish hillsides, nature is near at hand. To be within earshot of curlews and within a rod's length of kingfisher and dipper is repayment enough for not being somewhere else more famous, better publicised, and almost certainly more expensive.

THE NYMPH

Between dry fly and wet fly lies nymph-fishing, the celebrated 'Minor Tactics' of G. E. M. Skues. Here the principle is not to imitate with a floating fly the natural insect in its winged state — the dun or spinner in angling parlance — but the nymph, or swimming pupa, as it ascends to the surface, there to wriggle out of its shuck, dry its wings and be airborne. The artificial nymph is cast upstream and sometimes 'worked' by manipulation of the rod to bring it upwards through the water in a natural manner, and to simulate life. There would appear to be no difference in principle between casting to a fish feeding below the water surface on natural prey an artificial version designed to deceive him, and casting an artificial floating fly to a fish taking its prey as it floats on the surface. Nevertheless views for and against the propriety of nymph-fishing caused a great stir for many years. Although the method is now almost universally accepted, the argument is not quite dead.

So much for the abstract, considered from the viewpoint of the trout-fisher. Before moving to the actual, the viewpoint must be widened to include the flyfisher's other game quarry — salmon, sea-trout and grayling.

SALMON, SEA-TROUT & GRAYLING

In Britain flyfishing for salmon equates with wet-fly fishing for trout with tackle reinforced for so powerful a quarry, and the difference that a single fly is customarily used for salmon instead of the normal 'team' of three as for trout. In North America dry-fly fishing for salmon has proved successful; though often tried, it has never established itself as a feasible method here.

Sea-trout also are normally fished for with a wet-fly downstream.

Some enthusiasts in some specially favourable places take them on dry fly, but the method is not usual, and is not advised, except in local conditions which offer overwhelming arguments in its favour. The nymph has no place as such in fishing for either salmon or sea-trout.

So, to grayling, Britain's most under-valued fish. It stands higher on the Continent. In France *l'ombre* (the shadow) is esteemed above trout both for sport and on the table, except in the chalkstream country of Normandy. This preference is probably longstanding. In England the alternative name for grayling, now archaic, was umber. Its obvious derivation from the French suggests that it may have been Norman in origin, after the conquest of 1066. The present existence of grayling in tributaries of the Severn, to which they are non-indigenous, is consistent with artificial transplanting of ova in the Middle Ages to make a delicacy familiar elsewhere available to newly arrived epicures.

Whether as delicacy or quarry, a misfortune has befallen grayling as a result of our close seasons for game fish. Because there has been no established British tradition of fishing for grayling for their own sake, our opinion of them has tended to come from those who have caught them as a by-product of fishing for trout. This has brought a dual malediction on grayling. When a fisherman has gone to great trouble, and some expense, to devote his utmost skill to catching a trout, only to find a grayling entering his landing net, he is not best pleased; especially when he takes a closer look at the grayling and finds it an unappetising sight.

This species spawns in spring. Therefore those that are caught in the legal season for trout are in fact kelts, and they look like it. Salmon and trout kelts are rightly regarded as unclean fish, and are protected by their close season dates. No such protection applies to grayling, since it could not be enforced without, in effect, preventing trout fishing. On the other hand, to fish for grayling in the autumn and early winter, which is close season for trout, remains legal. It is remarkable that few fishermen do this, especially as so many lament that the flyfishing season is too short, closes too early, and that the only thing wrong with the sport is that it cannot be followed in the cooler months.

Thanks to grayling it can be. They rise well to the upstream dry-fly, and there are few days even in mid-winter when there is no natural hatch, if only for an hour or so, failing which the upstream nymph in practised hands generally succeeds. From October onwards, when the sunlit air is cooling and bonfire smoke from cottage gardens drifts across the stream, when the nip of approaching winter invigorates the fisherman and the ordeal of procreation is long forgotten by the fish, the grayling is a very different creature. Thickened now, broad of shoulder, firm muscled, and scenting the air aromatically as befits its Latin name *Thymallus*, it gives its captor his reward both in the water and on the plate. No fish which has had so many evocative names is likely to be a side-issue, and it is time to stop regarding the grayling as one. It is a fish of fast water, and of pure water. It cannot live without flow, and the consequent high level of oxygenation. A stream fit for grayling is most certainly fit for the more discerning fishermen.

PUTTING THEORY INTO PRACTICE

He who wishes to fish rivers must make many choices. None is more important than the simple, Which? Many factors will enter into it, including those of accessibility and cost which are personal to each individual. So it will now be assumed that a fisherman in spirit, but not yet in fact, has elected to make his debut on a stream which, holding both trout and grayling, is suitable for the wet fly. He is an informed but not specialised naturalist. He has become inclined towards fly fishing through reading some of the classics of the sport so he knows at secondhand its spirit, its essentials, and its language. Having also read the other chapters in this book he has mastered his tackle and is fully equipped. Lest a hatch of olives or a fall of spinner turn the eyes of every trout skyward, he has another rod made up with dry-fly line and leader.

He is standing there where once I stood, in the same state of theoretical knowledge, great expectations, and considerable humility (though less well equipped), my first cast on water yet to be made. The Teme ripples out of the border hills; Shropshire's sweet green grass laps the red earth banks. Behind him that lean grey watcher of a troubled frontier, Ludlow Castle, stares dead-eyed into Wales.

Unknown quantity though each new river is, at least it tells us one thing. We know which way the fish are facing, which is more than the wisest man knows on a still water. It would help to know also where the fish are. We cannot gain this knowledge by looking for it, because the Teme, like most wet-fly water, has a dark bed and a broken surface. So we read the water. What looks at first like a disorganised flow proves on closer examination to have a pattern to it. Two streams part company at a projecting stone, flow side by side for ten yards until one plaits over the other, and the pace slackens. The line of bubbles marking the main stream leaves a large area of flat water between itself and the left bank, where a cattle drink is wired off. Further down, where the flow begins to speed again, the surface is broken into sharp little waves culminating in a hump with a dip behind it. So much for the evidence, now for the interpretation.

If we could look at a river surface in section, from about eye-level, we should see that even when not rippled by wind it is seldom flat. It curves and swells like the muscles of a man's back. These features result from deflections in the flow where the moving water is thrust upwards or sideways by objects on the bed. A large stone will be reflected by a hump at the surface a yard or so downstream of its actual position. Smaller stones produce surface wavelets.

33. Clues and deductions in reading a river. *The flow is presented in section, the water moves left to right. (a) A smooth-bedded pool indicated by smooth flow above. (b) Surface 'popple' results from a stony bed where flow accelerates. (c) The hump at the surface caused by a boulder below. (d) The boulder's downstream eddy where a trout might lie.*

It is immediately below a large stone that a trout may be expected to lie in wait for food. Protected from the main force of the river, it rests almost without effort in the eddy. Only a good sized fish will be man enough to hold so desirable a position, especially if it lies below the confluence of two of the river's component streams, for they will bring a double supply line of food to the tenant of the lie. Fish will not lie in wait (though may idly cruise) in the dead water between the bubbles and the bank.

What the fisherman must now do is to bring his flies sideways and slowly into the field of view of a trout lying behind the stone. By casting across and downstream, at about 45° to the opposite bank, he will achieve this as the stream sweeps his line downstream and causes it to cover an arc of the river bed as it goes. This simplistic approach demands adjustment to different conditions. If the flow is heavy after recent spate a cast of 45° may bring the flies across too fast and too high in the water. By casting, say, at a 30° angle to the opposite bank, the current will gain less of a hold on the line; it will therefore be moved less rapidly across the stream to the point immediately below the rod-tip where lateral movement ceases, and the flies will have proportionately longer in which to sink to the best fishing depth. Alternatively, low water may leave a river slack and lifeless so that its flow imparts too little movement to the flies. In this case the cast is made nearer 90° to the opposite bank. The stream can then bring whatever force it possesses to bear upon the whole length of the line, first putting a downstream bight into it, then straightening it out, the whole process accelerating the movement of the flies.

Unless the flies are in fact moving, and held by leader and droppers so that they face into the flow of water, they are said not to be 'fishing'. Only if the water activates the dressing does the artificial fly gain that quality of liveliness which momentarily persuades a trout that here is a creature to be eaten. If merely bowled along inert in the current, as when a slack line is being straightened, they lack all shape and impulsion, resembling debris. In this state, however, they sink in the absence of lift from the tension of the line, and this fact is used to lower flies which are riding too high by means of an upstream 'mend', which is a way of saying that more line is flicked into the current above the flies in order to create an interval while the stream straightens it out; in this interval the flies sink lower.

Assuming the conventional team of three flies, opinions differ as to the principle governing their choice. Most fishermen, myself included, give much thought to abstruse considerations such as whether, given Grouse and Green on the bob and Claret and Mallard on the point, the dropper position should be allocated to Woodcock and Yellow (having regard to the possibility of thunder, the slight cloudiness of the water reported at the inn, and so on) or to something else. To me this is part of the unnecessary fuss without which flyfishing would be less than half the fun. Every Englishman is a selector at heart, and to be able to pick a team fortifies the ego. But I am unconvinced that it makes much difference to the catching of fish, however great its entertainment value. Three Grouse and Greens, since each would be at a different level in the water, would probably give equal results.

As the flies sweep round towards the surface hump which indicates the submerged stone, momentarily imagine that, instead of the innocent Teme stream, the might cataract of Awe is flowing. Well-named, indeed, for it is an awesome sight as it plunges from its parent loch the short six miles to salt water. With the breast of Tervine above him to the left, and the huge bulk of Ben Cruachan on the right, a man is well cut down to size. Instead of the gentle Shropshire vale, tuneful with its gurgles and tinkles, there is a boulder-stacked canyon in which the river roars. There are savage boils, plumes of white water, and sudden flats covering depth enough to drown in. Instead of ten yards of river bed, the fisherman must think of fifty.

But in essence a cast's length of the Teme contains it all in miniature. The man who has known small streams can read large rivers, and fish them sensibly. If a salmon takes, the thrill of the moment will be supreme. But there is no monopoly in supremacy, and a 12-ounce trout from the lie behind the stone on Teme would be no whit inferior.

THE TAKE

No man can speak other than personally. So my experience may be very exceptional in that of the hundreds of trout which I have caught very, very few have left me a memory of the actual rise to the fly and the hooking of them. Nothing separates the moment in which I am still hoping from the moment when a fish is on and the fight has started. The process seems comparable to falling from a horse, in which the actual descent is seldom remembered and the dislodged rider is aware only of the aftermath of impact. In short, the shock of hooking a fish, like that of hitting the ground, obliterates the memory's record of the preceding second or so. The result is that the fisherman's crucial part in tightening to a risen fish, and thus driving home the hook, depends on reflexes of which he is unaware, but which depend on his mental and physical characteristics.

Flyfishing is a sport in which considerable strength must sometimes be exerted momentarily and precisely, timing being more important than force. In the hooking of fish I do not personally regard the verb 'strike' as helpful or accurate, since it implies too much the element of attack, and too little the element of response. It must never be forgotten that it is from the fish, not from the fisherman, that all the actuating decisions come. The fish takes the initiative of attacking the fly, the fisherman answers by (he hopes) hooking the fish, and the action is as automatic and unpremeditated, yet disciplined and practised as a cricketer making a late cut.

Cricketer's eye and cricketer's wrist, not to mention cricketer's quickness, give trout fishing an premium to the young and, less often recognised than might be thought, to the feminine. The beauty and sensitivity of a fly rod as a sporting weapon adds its effect. Though comparisons are odious some are inescapable and

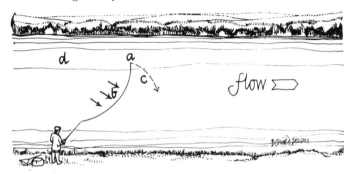

WET FLY: (a) *The fisherman drops his flies downstream towards the far bank.* (b) *His line, at first straight, is moved by the flow of the river.* (c) *His flies move sideways through the places where trout may lie.* (d) *Dead water, where feeding fish would not be expected.*

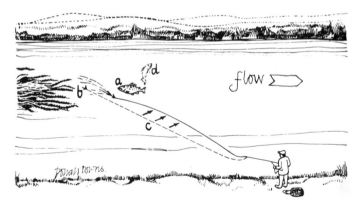

DRY FLY: (a) *The target trout, feeding below trailing weeds.* (b) *The fly has been cast on a straight line, cross-current.* (c) *The current snatches the line and drags the fly unnaturally across it.* (d) *The trout has seen it all before, and exits fast.*
34. Drag, a help in wet-fly and a problem in dry-fly fishing.

after forty years of flyfishing I now know all too well that at I am likely to be excelled by three classes of person. First by any experienced fisher two decades or more my junior; secondly, by an athletic, country-wise young woman; thirdly, by a Frenchman. The margins are that time blunts the reflexes; that a woman's touch has its place in flyfishing; and that Frenchmen, besides heirs to a great angling tradition, are the world's greatest realists and so make themselves complete masters of anything they undertake or else give it up. This is especially so on a chalk stream, where the trout are large, visible and numerous. So large that zest for possession clouds the judgement, so visible that every spot and each pulsation of the gills proclaims the prospect of capture, so numerous that every cast must be planned like a snooker shot to steer the line between them and to avoid scaring some lesser fish whose movement would cause a general exodus. The womanly caution against a gambling throw, and the Gallic gift of patience score heavily there where the dry flyfisher's bane of 'drag' dominates every calculation.

DRAG

Drag is the effect of the weight of the stream exerted against a floating line, pulling the fly sideways across the current exactly as

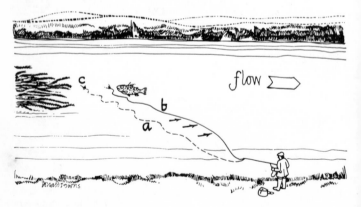

35. Counteracting drag with the dry-fly. (a) *This time the line has skilfully been case loose.* (b) *The water flow takes time to straighten the curves.* (c) *So the fly floats over the trout before the line can drag it.*

happens under water in wet-fly fishing. There it is the energising factor which gives pseudo-life to the artificial fly. On the surface it is the give-away which reveals the artificial fly for what it is, for no natural fly can move sideways across a current, and every trout well knows it. The answer to drag is to cast from such a position below the target fish that it does not happen — which is tantamount to saying that the way to win at chess is to defeat the opposition. It can be done, but not always.

At salmon I would expect to hold my own. The tempo is slower, the scene is wider; the ratio of strength to skill is greater; the distractions and the physical odds more pressing; the location almost certainly more remote; the cost greater, and the element of luck greater still. A man fishing badly may catch a salmon, but not very often. A man fishing brilliantly may not catch a salmon for weeks on end either because there have been no fish there, or that the fish which have been there were not taking at the moment when his fly passed through the lie. But to catch a salmon is too rewarding an experience ever to be foregone.

Flyfishing swings from small beginnings to high moments and back again. We live in an unprecedented era of big trout on the huge new still waters, of new standards in sizes and numbers in the catch at the end of the day, of new emphasis in publicity, of unabated water abstraction and threats of pollution. Yet the streams still flow, men are still ready to defend them, and to treasure as much as ever they did their modest rewards for having taken on not merely the fish but the river as well, with all its defensive secrets.

Index

128

Index